Today's Debates

HEALTH CARE

Universal Right or Personal Responsibility?

Corinne J. Naden and Erin L. McCoy

Cavendish
Square

New York

Published in 2019 by Cavendish Square Publishing, LLC
243 5th Avenue, Suite 136, New York, NY 10016

Library of Congress Cataloging-in-Publication Data

Names: Naden, Corinne J., author. | McCoy, Erin L., author.
Title: Health care : universal right or personal responsibility? / Corinne J. Naden and Erin L. McCoy.
Description: First edition. | New York : Cavendish Square, 2019. | Series:
Today's debates | Audience: Grades 7-12. | Includes bibliographical
references and index.
Identifiers: LCCN 2018014936 (print) | LCCN 2018017207 (ebook) | ISBN
9781502643278 (ebook) | ISBN 9781502643261 (library bound) |
ISBN 9781502643254 (pbk.)
Subjects: LCSH: Medical policy--United States--Juvenile literature. | Medical
care--United States--Juvenile literature. | National health
insurance--United States--Juvenile literature.
Classification: LCC RA395.A3 (ebook) | LCC RA395.A3 N2856 2019 (print) | DDC 362.10973--dc23
LC record available at https://lccn.loc.gov/2018014936

Editorial Director: David McNamara
Copy Editor: Rebecca Rohan
Associate Art Director: Alan Sliwinski
Production Coordinator: Karol Szymczuk
Photo Research: J8 Media

Printed in the United States of America

CONTENTS

Introduction 5

Chapter One: Providing Health Care 13

Chapter Two: Paying for Health Care 33

Chapter Three: Regulating Health Care 47

Chapter Four: Key Controversies 61

Chapter Five: Pharmaceuticals and the Law 75

Chapter Six: Health Care Around the World 89

Chapter Seven: The Future of Health Care 103

Glossary 126

Further Information 128

Bibliography 131

Index 140

About the Authors 144

INTRODUCTION

The question of whether the United States needs or even wants universal health-care coverage has been at the forefront of political debate for decades, brought to a head by the passage of the Patient Protection and Affordable Care Act in 2010. Since then, the country's two major parties have been battling over whether to maintain, repeal, or replace this law, which requires that most (but not all) Americans have health-care coverage. Fundamental questions about the right to health care have been at play, alongside debates about the role of government, the right to privacy, and the cost of health care.

How the United States Stacks Up

The Affordable Care Act addressed what many saw as key flaws in the US health-care system. However, many disagree that such flaws exist.

Opposite: Everyone needs health care—but how such care is administered and paid for in the United States has been up for debate for decades.

For years, some politicians and insurance companies have boasted that US health care is the best in the world. They point out that waiting times to see specialists or enter a hospital are shorter than almost anywhere else. They cite the availability of medicines and the ongoing medical research that brings new cures and new methods of treatment to thousands of patients.

Others argue that the United States' health-care system doesn't measure up to those of other developed countries. Millions of Americans are without health insurance at all. Health insurance allows people to pay money a little at a time, usually once a month, to ensure that they'll pay much less than the sticker price when they need routine and emergency procedures. In 2010, before the passage of the Affordable Care Act, 49 million Americans—16.3 percent of the population—were without health insurance. That figure dropped to 28.1 million Americans, or 8.8 percent of Americans, in 2016, according to the US Census Bureau—an improvement, though many argue it's still not enough. In comparison, only about 5 percent of people in France don't have voluntary coverage, and in the Netherlands less than 1 percent of residents are uninsured.

Meanwhile, health-care outcomes in the United States often don't measure up to those of other countries. In comparison with the world's twenty richest countries, the United States ranked worst for child mortality, with US-born babies 76 percent more likely to die before reaching one year of age than babies born in other countries. What's more, access to care in the United States was ranked worse than that of any other countries when compared to ten other developed nations in a 2016 Commonwealth Fund survey. Thirty-three percent of Americans surveyed did not visit a doctor, skipped tests, or did not take their medication due to cost. Many Americans who are covered by health insurance still can't afford to pay for the prescription drugs they need. All of this is true despite the fact that the United States spends more on health care per capita than any other nation—twice as much as Australia, France, Japan, and the United Kingdom.

Critics of the system also point out that the United States is the only major country in the world that does not look upon health care as a major right of its citizens. Instead, it is a service or commodity to be purchased by consumers. As a result, many Americans with preexisting medical conditions that were expensive to treat were denied coverage until the Affordable Care Act made this illegal.

The Shifting Debate

The last few years have seen a significant shift in how Americans view the health-care debate. In 2013—the year before the Affordable Care Act was fully implemented—just 42 percent of Americans believed that the government is responsible for ensuring that all citizens are covered, yet 60 percent believed this in 2017. As Sarah Kliff points out in an article for *Vox*, "An 18-point swing in just four years is a remarkably fast change in the world of public policy polling." In the same 2017 poll, government-provided health programs such as Medicaid also tended to poll higher than private coverage supported by subsidies. The latter have seen support among lawmakers who oppose government having a large role in providing health-care services, arguing that such programs might mean higher costs and breaches of personal privacy.

How the US health-care system will ultimately be structured remains far from certain. Taking a look at other countries' health-care systems can offer insight into the most and least effective ways of balancing private and public insurance and health-care services, and of instituting an effective universal health-care system—if one should be implemented at all. Let's take a look at health care and health coverage (insurance) in the United States and around the world to better understand every side of this tumultuous and multifaceted debate.

Chapter One

PROVIDING HEALTH CARE

When the Patient Protection and Affordable Care Act was passed in 2010, many Americans were up in arms. The Republican Party argued that it would result in higher insurance costs, higher taxes, and fewer health-care options. Republicans gained the majority in the US House of Representatives in 2011 over the Democratic party, which had passed the Affordable Care Act under President Barack Obama. Between 2011 and 2014, Republicans voted fifty-four times to dismantle or revamp the law, with no success. When President Barack Obama faced reelection in 2012, the *Washington Post* declared the law, nicknamed Obamacare, the "most important issue of this election."

Opposite: US president Barack Obama signs the Patient Protection and Affordable Care Act at the White House on March 23, 2010.

The issue was up for debate again during the 2016 presidential election, after which newly elected Republican president Donald Trump and a Republican-majority Congress sought to "repeal and replace" the law. Several such measures ultimately failed by a narrow margin, and the closest Congress had come as of early 2018 was a repeal of the individual mandate, which requires that Americans buy insurance or else pay a penalty. Democrats argue that the mandate is essential for keeping health care affordable under the Obamacare model.

Whatever form health insurance coverage takes in the coming years, the American health-care system will remain a complex web of organizations, companies, programs, research facilities, pharmaceutical companies, and health-care professionals, each with their own roles to play. In order to understand the debate over health care, it is first essential to learn about how the American health-care system operates.

Types of Health Care

Health care in the United States is a crazy quilt of different medical plans and services. An American who needs medical attention or coverage faces a bewildering list of people, institutions, organizations, plans, and practices. There are primary care physicians, hospitals and hospices; nursing homes and home health-care programs; drug companies and insurance companies; ambulatory care sites; and managed-care plans. Meanwhile, Medicare and Medicaid are government-issued programs for older and low-income Americans.

Even with all of these systems in place, the United States, unlike most major industrialized nations, does not guarantee health care to all its citizens. Most Germans have been covered by a health-care system since the 1880s. Great Britain adopted the National Health Service (NHS), the world's first government-provided universal system, in 1948. Canada has universal health coverage, and so do Brazil, Costa Rica, Japan, and Cuba, among other nations.

There are several types of health care available in the United States based on a person's particular condition or need. Health-care offerings are also categorized according to special groups that they serve, such as veterans and the elderly.

Outpatient Care

Most health care in the United States takes place on an outpatient basis—that is, in a doctor's office or clinic where patients don't spend the night. Americans who are covered by health insurance generally visit a primary-care physician (PCP), also called a general practitioner (GP), for basic health needs. The doctor may refer the patient to a specialist, such as a gastroenterologist (who treats digestive organs) or a cardiologist (a heart specialist). Some health plans allow the patient to go directly to a specialist. In some regions, often in rural areas or inner cities, the patient may see a health provider who is not a physician but a nurse practitioner or physician's assistant. Depending on their level of education, these health-care providers can treat illnesses, prescribe certain medications, and even perform some minor surgeries.

Many medical procedures don't require a hospital visit. Outpatient care—also called ambulatory care—is fine for such procedures as X-ray imaging or blood tests. For some procedures, such as the setting of a broken arm, a patient may receive ambulatory care in a hospital.

Sometimes, people go to hospital emergency rooms (ERs) for what turns out to be ambulatory care—a fever or severe rash, for instance. These are often people who don't have health insurance and therefore don't have primary-care physicians with whom they can make appointments. As many as 33 percent of Americans choose not to visit a doctor, skip tests, or do not take their medication because of high costs, and as a result, many end up in the ER once otherwise manageable medical conditions have become more serious. Although some emergency room visits do require admission to the hospital, 92 percent do not.

Some patients receive outpatient treatment in urgent-care centers. These centers are designed to treat ailments not severe enough for hospital admission. However, some patients may need to be treated quickly or at times when the doctor's office is closed. For instance, a patient may visit an urgent-care center in the early morning hours complaining of a severe earache.

Outpatient care is also available for students in their schools and on college campuses, and for inmates in US prisons. Visits to the dentist, eye doctor, or dermatologist (skin specialist) are also usually on an outpatient basis.

A new and somewhat controversial concept in personal health care arose in the late 1990s. It is generally called concierge, boutique, or retainer medicine. It means that a consumer gets personal care and attention from a primary-care physician. For instance, if a concierge patient gets the flu, his or her doctor may make a home visit instead of the patient going to the doctor's office. The patient may have around-the-clock access to the doctor, including the doctor's cell phone number, which is not generally the case in most doctor-patient relationships. What's more, the concierge patient never has to wait in a crowded reception room.

This level of service is not cheap; in fact, it is primarily available only to the wealthy. For example, a concierge patient may pay a $2,000 yearly fee, and some fees are much higher. This is in addition to the amount he or she may pay in Medicare premiums or copays (the portion of a charge that the patient pays). Some concierge doctors don't take insurance.

Not very many US physicians offer this kind of care, although there are boutique doctors from New York to California. One drawback is that it limits the number of patients a doctor can see.

That's why some doctors give regular as well as concierge care. While this may seem like it would stretch a doctor's time very thin, the American Medical Association has said that this trend does not violate medical ethics as long as "those paying such an extra fee and those who are not … get an equal quality of care from that practitioner."

Another form of medical care, called direct primary care, has emerged in response to the Affordable Care Act and the difficulties that doctors face when it comes to insurance requirements. This more affordable form of concierge service costs about $100 per month and gives patients direct access to their general practitioners and basic medication. The approach gives doctors relief from excessive paperwork, which many say has been exacerbated by Obamacare. The number of direct primary care practices increased from six to twenty in 2010 to more than four hundred in 2016.

A number of other professionals form part of the outpatient health-care spectrum. For instance, some pharmacies are hiring health providers such as nurse practitioners to make periodic store visits to see patients with medical problems. Pharmacists not only handle prescription drugs, but now also administer flu shots and vaccines at the drugstores where they work; no doctor's appointment is needed. Sometimes a doctor schedules health-care services that not only involve skilled nurses, but social workers, health aides, and physical, speech, or occupational therapists. These people may work in hospitals, clinics, offices, or the patient's home.

Social workers help people with problems. They might counsel a family with a gravely ill relative about care options. They might try to find shelter for a homeless person. Child, family, and school social workers may seek out foster homes for abused or homeless children. Medical and public health social workers advise people who have longtime health problems. Mental health and substance abuse social workers counsel those with mental illness or alcohol abuse problems.

Personal and home health-care aides help the elderly, physically disabled, and mentally disabled. They work in the patients' homes or in health-care facilities and institutions. They may work in one home for months or even longer, and their duties vary according to need. These aides generally work on their own with periodic visits from a supervisor, who may be a registered nurse, physical therapist, or social worker.

Physical therapists help people with limited or permanent disability generally caused by injury or disease. Treatment often involves some type of exercise as well as electrical stimulation to relieve pain. Speech therapists work with those who have difficulty speaking, sometimes as the result of a brain injury. Occupational therapists work with patients who suffer from a physically or developmentally disabling condition, such as a spinal cord injury or muscular dystrophy. Their main aim is to help patients learn to tend to their own daily needs.

Hospital Care

Hospitals are relatively large institutions that treat patients whose medical problems can't be treated in a doctor's office. Heart surgery, for example, must be performed in a hospital. In addition to surgeries, patients may go to the hospital to give birth or to receive care for a bad drug reaction or an automobile accident injury. The two main types of hospitals in the United States are nonprofit and for-profit.

Most US hospitals are nonprofit. This means that they must serve some public purpose, which in turn affords them special treatment under the law, such as property tax and income tax exemptions. Despite the name, nonprofit hospitals can make a profit (and many do); they just can't be designed primarily for that purpose. Some nonprofit hospitals have ties

Physical therapists help those people who, because of a short-term or permanent disability, suffer mobility problems or related pain.

to religious institutions. They may be governed by religious leaders or run by, for instance, nuns from the Sisters of Charity or other religious orders.

A for-profit hospital is usually operated by a private corporation. These investor-owned institutions, which became more common in the late twentieth century, are set up to bring in a profit for their shareholders. They claim that, with their emphasis on efficiency, they can offer better care at a lower cost than the nonprofit sector. HCA Healthcare is the largest of this type. It is based in Nashville, Tennessee, and runs almost 170 hospitals throughout the United States and the United Kingdom.

Detractors of for-profit hospitals say they are successful because they mainly serve the wealthy and avoid areas where they would have to treat poorer populations. They claim that these institutions specialize in such expensive procedures as elective plastic surgery and avoid unprofitable services like emergency medicine.

Probably the busiest place in a hospital is the ER. People go to the ER for sudden medical emergencies, such as heart attacks or severe allergic reactions. They will also visit an ER if they are away from home and cannot reach their own physician. The emergency room at any hospital is usually identified by a prominent sign, often combining red and white as recognizable colors for this type of medical care.

The term "emergency room," however, is actually a misnomer. The modern hospital may have several rooms or areas to be used for emergency cases. The first stop in an emergency room is usually the triage area. "Triage" is a French word that refers to the act of "sorting," which is what the triage nurse does. He or she determines the order in which patients should be seen based on the seriousness of each person's condition. A badly sprained ankle can wait, but a possible heart attack requires a doctor's attention right away. After triage, the patient may be sent to the general medical area, where people with all sorts of problems await medical attention. They may be assigned a bed, which is generally a gurney—a cot on wheels—rather than a hospital bed. Another key ER site is the trauma bay or trauma resuscitation area. It is stocked with oxygen tubes, defibrillator equipment to restore normal heart rhythms, and emergency drugs to regulate the heartbeat. Some ERs have a pediatric area for children. However, if a pregnant woman visits the ER, she will probably be sent directly to the hospital's obstetrics and maternity ward. Some ERs may also have a separate area for patients with psychiatric problems.

Patients generally either transport themselves to the hospital or arrive by ambulance. After being seen by the triage nurse, a walk-in patient is treated according to the seriousness of his or her condition, not the time of arrival. However, those who arrive by ambulance may be taken directly to the trauma bay if their condition is critical. An ambulance crew transporting a seriously ill patient will notify the ER that they are on the way and report on what they think is wrong. The patient may be met by a trauma team, which consists of doctors and nurses and, if necessary, a surgeon and an anesthesiologist.

Probably the biggest problem facing ERs in the United States, as well as in most other countries, is overcrowding. People often use the ER for nonemergency services. For instance, if someone injures his arm on a Sunday afternoon when his doctor's office is closed, he may go to the emergency room of his local hospital for treatment. Or, if a child develops an earache at three o'clock in the morning, her mother might take her to the ER. In both of these examples, people who have insurance and primary-care doctors may choose to use the ER only because, at the moment, they have nowhere else to go.

However, a main reason for overcrowding is the number of visits by people with low incomes and little or no insurance. Because they can't afford to have primary-care doctors, they tend to use the ER instead, even if a condition is not life-threatening.

Specialties

Some nonprofit hospitals are specialized or have specialty centers, such as St. Jude Children's Research Hospital, or the Center for Cardiovascular Disease in Women, based at Brigham and Women's Hospital in Boston, Massachusetts. The latter is dedicated to making women aware of heart disease and related complications.

Hospitals primarily exist for inpatient care. However, they do give outpatient care in emergency rooms and specialty clinics, such as a surgicenter. In this kind of facility, a patient is admitted early in the morning and is sedated for the surgery, which is sometimes elective. An elective surgery is one that need not be performed on an emergency basis because delaying it will not generally lead to unfavorable outcomes. For example, cosmetic surgery such as liposuction or rhinoplasty is usually elective. After

St. Jude Children's Research Hospital

A well-known example of a specialized institution is St. Jude Children's Research Hospital in Memphis, Tennessee. It was founded in 1962 by actor-comedian Danny Thomas and named for the Catholic patron saint of hospitals, Saint Jude Thaddeus. St. Jude treats children with cancer and other serious illnesses regardless of the family's ability to pay. Thomas also founded the American Lebanese Syrian Associated Charities (ALSAC), which is the fundraiser for St. Jude.

Patients come from all over the United States and many foreign countries to receive treatment at St. Jude. Depending on the illness and severity, there may be a waiting list for admission. The hospital sees about 7,500 patients each year; many are treated on an outpatient basis or participate in research programs. St. Jude also has eight affiliate clinics around the United States. At these clinics, patients have access to treatments that St. Jude has developed in clinical trials.

Work at St. Jude has helped to dramatically increase the survival rates of children suffering from devastating illnesses. For example, its doctors have helped to improve the survival rate for acute lymphoblastic leukemia (ALL). This disease of the white blood cells is the most common cancer in children. When St. Jude opened, the survival rate for children with ALL was less than 5 percent; today, ALL patients at St. Jude have a 94 percent survival rate. In 1996, Dr. Peter Doherty of St. Jude was named co-winner of the Nobel Prize in Physiology or Medicine for his work related to the immune system.

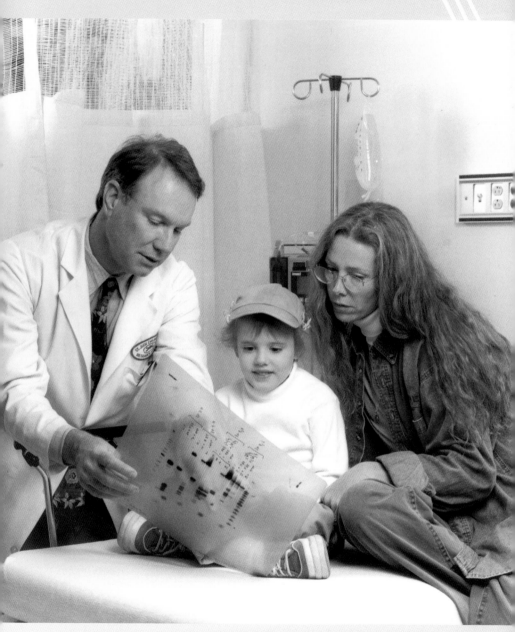

Dr. William Evans, deputy director of St. Jude, shows study results to a patient and her mother.

surgery, the patient is observed during the day until the anesthetic wears off, and he or she goes home later in the day escorted by a friend or relative. The Oral and Maxillofacial Surgery Professional Services Clinic at Baylor University in Dallas, Texas, is an example. In most cases, costs are reduced because no overnight stay is involved. Those with serious surgeries or whose health is questionable are not admitted. If complications occur after surgery in the Baylor clinic, the patient may be admitted to the Baylor University Medical Campus.

Instead of going to an ER for quick medical attention, a patient may go to an urgent-care center. First in existence in the 1970s, there are now about 7,100 around the country. These profit-oriented centers provide unscheduled, walk-in care. Patients generally need immediate attention for problems not serious enough to warrant a trip to the emergency room, such as a sprained ankle. Urgent care centers may also offer free blood-pressure checks to anyone or blood-sugar checks for diabetics on certain days. They generally accept all insurance plans, although programs for low-income Americans such as Medicaid are often not accepted. Those without insurance are charged a flat fee, usually ranging from about $90 to $150. Urgent-care centers are not generally open 24 hours a day; some may operate from 9:00 a.m. to 5:00 p.m. or on another fixed schedule.

Nursing Homes, Hospice, and Long-term Care

People who need constant attention and help with everyday living may be cared for in nursing homes, skilled nursing facilities, or skilled nursing units. Such patients include the elderly and younger adults with physical problems. Some people may spend their last years in a nursing home; others may be there for a short time to recover from a broken hip, for example. Medicare covers nursing-home stays for a very limited time and for limited purposes.

US nursing homes must always have a licensed nurse on duty. During at least one shift each day, the licensed nurse must be a registered nurse (RN). There are three types of registered nurses. Nurses with a BSN (Bachelor of Science in Nursing) have generally completed a four- or five-year program at a college or university. A nurse with an associate's degree has completed a two-year program, usually in a community college. The diploma nurse (more common before the 1970s) has usually completed a three-year program in a hospital. The staff may also include LPNs (licensed practical nurses), who have completed an accredited nursing program, usually at a technical or community college.

Hospice care is also known as end-of-life care. It is paid for by Medicare and is designed for those people judged to have six months or less to live and for those who have refused medical intervention. The care is given by health professionals (doctors and RNs) and the many, many volunteers who are vital to the program. Care can take place in the patient's home, a hospice center, a hospital, or a skilled nursing facility. Wherever the patient is, health professionals visit on a regular basis to check on medicines or dress wounds. Home visits might be scheduled for twice a week, for example. The professionals speak with their patients' families, advising them of their condition. Volunteers keep the hospice running by answering phones, keeping medical records, sitting and talking with patients when needed, and helping to ease what is usually a painful time for both patient and family.

Hospice services vary by state. Florida, for instance, has a comprehensive system. A patient who is being cared for at home can enter a hospice facility for just a few days if the home caregiver has to be absent or just needs a rest. Some states have too few hospice facilities to offer such an option. The aim of hospice care everywhere is to control pain and other distressing symptoms and to help people who are dying to do so in peace and with dignity.

Long-term care is for people who suffer from disabilities or chronic illnesses. It can be provided at home, in nursing homes, or at community facilities. It usually involves assisting people with daily living tasks, such as dressing and bathing. Each year,

Older people who need help on a daily basis often enter nursing homes or similar facilities.

millions of older Americans require long-term care of some kind—but people may need long-term care at any age.

Generally, Medicare pays for necessary skilled-nursing facilities or home health care. The person must be homebound to receive home health care and when that circumstance changes, the care is quickly terminated. Medicare does not pay for long-term care called custodial care, meaning help with daily activities, such as housekeeping.

Minors in the Health Care System

The number of uninsured people in the United States includes millions of children. According to the Kaiser Family Foundation, 5 percent of children in the United States are uninsured—more than 4.2 million in total.

Through the years, the US government has tried in various ways—and with varying degrees of success—to meet the health needs of children. In 1935, for instance, the Aid to Families with Dependent Children federal assistance program was created to provide financial assistance for needy families. At first, states gave cash payments to homes with only one parent. Later, two-parent homes were included if just one parent was working and the income was low. It was replaced in 1996 under US president Bill Clinton's administration by a cash welfare block grant called Temporary Assistance for Needy Families. These funds are used to get people off welfare and into jobs that could provide health coverage. President George W. Bush reauthorized it in 2005.

In 1997, during the Clinton administration, the Children's Health Insurance Program (CHIP) was created. It was the largest expansion of health-care coverage for children since Medicaid. This federal government program gives money to the states to cover families that cannot qualify for Medicaid funds. The states have some flexibility in how the program is run. The money may be used to expand Medicaid or it can be a separate program. Those states with separate programs have more flexibility than those that share Medicaid. They also may use different names such as Cub-Care in Maine or Dr. Dynasaur in Vermont.

Over the first two years, some one million children were enrolled in CHIP. However, in 2007, Congress twice tried to authorize expanding the CHIP budget. Both attempts were vetoed by President George W. Bush. He said that parents with more money might drop their own insurance for the better government option, thereby shifting the focus away from poor children.

During his presidential campaign, Obama vowed to revive the program. By 2010, some Democrats were proposing an end to CHIP, since the Affordable Care Act would have ideally covered low-income children. However, lawmakers defended the program, and today it covers about nine million children. In 2017, CHIP was threatened again as the Republican and Democratic parties struggled to reach a consensus on budget questions. A six-year extension of the program was signed in January 2018.

Through government contracts and private grants and endowments, all fifty states and numerous cities have varying degrees of health protection for children. Louisiana, for example, established the Louisiana Children's Code in 1992. It is aimed at protecting children whose physical or mental health needs are at risk, including victims of neglect. The code asserts the right to interfere in a family for the general welfare of the child. The city of Seattle, Washington, established the Center for Children with Special Needs in 1998. It focuses on children with chronic conditions such as asthma, autism, or cerebral palsy. It does not provide medical care but directs families to health professionals.

In all states, family planning and prenatal clinics offer services regardless of age or ability to pay. A family planning clinic usually provides birth control information, yearly medical exams, pregnancy counseling and tests, information on adoption and abortion, and screening for sexually transmitted diseases, including HIV tests.

One example is FPA Women's Health (formerly Family Planning Associates Medical Group) of California. It was founded in 1969, soon after abortion became legal in the state. The Supreme Court's 1973 decision in *Roe v. Wade* legalized abortion in all states. With *Roe v. Wade*, it also became legal to perform abortions outside the hospital. That made it possible for pregnancy and family planning services to be offered on an outpatient basis. FPA set up the state's first large outpatient pregnancy program in Santa Ana. Since then, the services of the FPA have increased, with twenty-four more facilities as far east as Chicago, Illinois. The FPA is now the largest independent family planning service in the country. Private-practice doctors as well as private and government agencies that do not want to perform abortions refer patients to FPA. Listed in its services are tests for pregnancy, abortions, birth control information, and sterilization procedures. The doctors who provide these services practice only for the FPA.

Many cities and states run teen clinics with services aimed at low-income, sexually active teenagers. All the services are confidential; the teens are not required to get parental permission for birth control or pregnancy tests. However, most of these clinics encourage teens to talk with the parents or trusted adults about any related problems. An example is Chicago's public health clinic, which opened a special program for teens in 1982. The idea grew

Chicago medical students rally for the reauthorization of the Children's Health Insurance Program two months after its funding expired in 2017.

out of the observations of the staff at the main clinic. They decided there was a need for a private place where teens could discuss their sexual or medical problems and get advice and help.

Most teen clinics are walk-ins. The teen just has to show up during the clinic's working hours. Some clinics, however, offer appointment times. No one is turned away because he or she cannot pay. Teen clinics can be found online in all major and most large US cities.

Prenatal clinics offer obstetric care to women regardless of ability to pay. The Pregnancy Center & Clinic of the Low Country in Jasper County, South Carolina, cares for women who are uninsured or underinsured and for those who don't qualify for Medicaid. Prenatal clinics provide tests for pregnancy and sexually transmitted diseases, clothing and equipment for infants, psychological counseling, adoption information, and prenatal care through the sixteenth week of gestation (normal pregnancy usually lasts forty weeks).

The Baby TALK (Teaching Activities for Learning and Knowledge) program was founded in Decatur, Illinois, in 1986, to develop healthy parent-child relationships during the critical early years. It operates in more than thirty-six states. Low-income parents and parents-to-be get counseling and education at the clinics. The program encourages literacy workshops and provides information about how children develop. It also offers hands-on treatment. Parents are invited to bring their new babies to the public library where they are introduced to the children's book section. The staff periodically makes phone calls to find out how the parents are coping with stress. If there is a problem, the staff can refer the parent to an agency that can help. If necessary, the Baby TALK staff makes home visits. The whole idea is to give the new parents confidence in their ability to take care of their own children.

Military and Veterans

The United States also provides health care to its domestic military personnel, retirees, and dependents, on military facilities, and in active war areas. There are multiple plans, including some especially for those who are overseas, for young adults, and for retired Reserve members.

US military veterans are covered by the United States Department of Veterans Affairs (VA), which was established in 1988 to replace the old Veterans Administration. The VA is the government's second-largest department after the Department of Defense. There are about 1,240 VA medical centers, offices, facilities, and clinics nationwide. The Veterans Health Administration is the branch responsible for providing health care to veterans.

If a veteran has a service-connected disability of 50 percent or higher (determined by the rating boards of VA regional offices), he or she receives care and medications at no charge. The veteran may also receive a pension, rated on the severity of the disability. Those with less severe or nonservice-connected health problems—those needing medication for asthma, for instance—are charged significantly reduced fees for their medications.

Native Peoples

Health care for federally recognized Native American tribes (numbering more than five hundred) and Alaska natives (including the Aleut) is the responsibility of the Indian Health Service (IHS). Part of the Department of Health and Human Services, it was established in 1955 to replace the Bureau of Indian Affairs. Hospitals and clinics run by the IHS give care to any registered Native American or Alaska native tribe members; health-care facilities on reservations serve only their own tribal members.

In 1976, the Indian Health Care Improvement Act was enacted. It is aimed at eliminating what some call a health-care crisis for this part of the population. The bill allocated about $35 million to be spent over the next ten years on building and improving clinics on reservations. It also called for recruiting more Native Americans into the health-care field. The Senate bill excluded abortions at most Native American health clinics. The act expired in 2000 but was permanently reauthorized as part of the Patient Protection and Affordable Care Act in 2010. It will remain in place as long as the Affordable Care Act does.

Special-Interest Groups

A special-interest group is an organized set of people who aim to influence political policy. They do not seek election to public office. There are many special-interest groups in the United States. For example, Greenpeace is concerned with the environment, and the National Rifle Association (NRA) focuses on laws related to the possession of firearms. One of the largest and most powerful special-interest groups in health care is the AARP.

The AARP was founded by Dr. Ethel Percy Andrus in 1958. A former high school principal, she had founded the National Retired Teachers Association in 1947 to help retired teachers get health insurance. A few years later, the group was opened to those over age fifty. Originally the American Association of Retired Persons, the name was changed to AARP in 1999. The change indicates that it does not focus solely on the retired. In fact, a person must be older than fifty but does not have to be retired to be a member.

AARP is a nongovernment special-interest group with almost thirty-eight million members. It addresses issues that are important to older Americans. It claims not to support or give money to candidates of any political party. It does, however, lobby on state and national issues.

The members of AARP have access to a number of services and products. It is a secondary health insurer to Medicare. Members pay a monthly premium for a plan that generally picks up the fees that Medicare does not pay. Members also receive discounts on such things as vacation packages or rental cars. Programs of the AARP Foundation help low-income, older workers with such tasks as preparing their taxes or job training.

Despite all these services, AARP is not without its critics. Some claim that the interests of AARP can conflict with the interests of its members. They say that members could get better and cheaper insurance policies on their own. AARP admits that its policies are not always the cheapest but feels that it offers a better deal overall than other policies.

Research Funding

Research funding generally refers to any money given for scientific research. The government, corporations, and foundations run what is essentially a competition. Potential research projects are evaluated, and since money is always scarce, only the most promising get funding. The two biggest sources of research funding in the United States are the government—through universities and specialized agencies—and the development departments of corporations. Some research money comes from charitable foundations that may want to develop cures for certain diseases.

The main agency for biomedical and health-related research in the United States is the National Institutes of Health (NIH). As part of the Department of Health and Human Services, the NIH invests more than $32 billion per year in medical research, funding more than three hundred thousand researchers throughout the country and almost six thousand in its own facilities.

NIH began back in 1887 as the Laboratory of Hygiene. In 1930, it was reorganized into the National Institute (singular) of Health. Today, it has twenty-seven separate centers and institutes. The institutes operate in various health areas. For instance, the National Institute of Environmental Health Sciences in North Carolina sponsors programs for students interested in careers in biomedical and biological sciences. The National Institute of Allergy and Infectious Diseases in Maryland studies all aspects of such infectious diseases as malaria, influenza, and AIDS. Other institutes look into aging, cancer, alcohol abuse, arthritis and skin diseases, eye diseases, and the structure of the human gene.

An example of a private research facility free of government restraints is the Howard Hughes Medical Institute in Chevy Chase, Maryland. It was founded in 1953 by aviator and engineer Howard Hughes. Today, it is one of the country's largest private organizations dedicated to funding medical and biological research. In 2017, it invested $662 million in biomedical research and $86 million in science education. Since Hughes's death in 1976, the institute has focused mainly on genetics (how traits and qualities are passed from parents to children), immunology (the study of disease and how the body responds to it), and molecular biology, which is chiefly concerned with understanding how various systems of a cell interact.

Chapter Two

PAYING FOR HEALTH CARE

Health care was a contentious issue during the 2016 US presidential elections as then–Republican candidate Donald Trump declared the Affordable Care Act a "disaster" and Democratic candidate Hillary Clinton vowed to protect the program and remedy some of its problems, including high premiums. Senator Bernie Sanders, a one-time frontrunner for the Democratic nomination, went a step further, advocating for a single-payer system which involves just one insurance provider—the government—rather than having multiple, competing insurance companies, referred to as a multi-payer system.

Opposite: Health care is a huge expense, and much of the debate surrounding it relates to how individuals and nations can pay for it.

Comparing Countries

Most wealthy, industrialized countries—including Germany, Belgium, and the Netherlands—have a single- or multi-payer system. Canada's system is single-payer and France's almost is, whereas Switzerland has a subsidized private model akin to Obamacare. Among wealthy nations, the United States is the only one to have an entirely private system in the form of employer-provided health coverage. As president, Trump has compared the United States' health-care system favorably with those of Europe. In a February 5, 2018 tweet, Trump insisted that the United Kingdom's system "is going broke and not working." Democrats, he added, "want to greatly raise taxes for really bad and non-personal medical care." Indeed, early 2018 saw excessively long waits and overcrowding due to staff shortages at British medical facilities after the UK's National Health Service experienced budget cuts.

Sanders, however, would continue to argue—this time in a 2017 article in British newspaper the *Guardian*—that the United States' health system couldn't stand up to those of comparable nations. "I live in Burlington, Vermont, 50 miles [80 kilometers] south of the Canadian border. For decades, every man, woman and child in Canada has been guaranteed healthcare through a single-payer health coverage program. In fact, universal health coverage exists in every wealthy industrialized country on earth, except the United States … It's time we joined the rest of the industrialized world in that regard," Sanders wrote.

He pointed to the relatively high cost of health care in the United States and the relatively poor outcomes. The United States has the world's most expensive health-care system by a wide margin. The Organization for Economic Cooperation and Development (OECD) reports that the United States spent $9,892 per capita on health care in 2016—a 45 percent

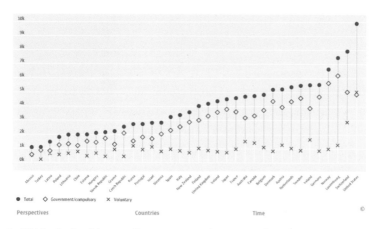

In 2016, the health spending per capita (per person) in the United States exceeded that of all other countries.

increase from just ten years before. The next highest spender was Switzerland, at $7,919 per capita.

Some might argue that higher US spending is a good thing. Don't you get what you pay for? Switzerland spent $1,973 less per person than the United States in 2016. But Switzerland's health-care system, according to a 2017 Commonwealth Fund analysis of eleven comparable, developed nations, was ranked sixth, whereas the United States was ranked last. The United Kingdom was ranked number one, but the British spent $5,700 less per person in 2016 than the United States. Are Americans really getting what they pay for?

Why do Americans spend so much? There seems to be several reasons. The costs of new medical technology and prescription drugs are constantly on the rise. The amount of paperwork that keeps the system running is staggering—and costly. More people live to older ages in the United States, which means more people need medical attention at some time. The uninsured are also a big reason for increased costs. When they need medical help, they often go to emergency rooms where costs are high but can be subsidized. If the uninsured don't seek help at all, their conditions may worsen, and they could end up needing intensive or long-term care treatment—again, very expensive.

Most Americans used to receive medical insurance through their employers. However, that is changing. Whereas 61.5 percent of Americans had employer-provided health-care coverage in 1989, that had decreased to 55.9 percent in 2004, and to 49 percent in 2016. Employer coverage has been steadily increasing in cost at a rate of about 3 percent per year as of 2017, and as a result, many employers are offering lower-quality plans. Many of these costs are passed on to employees in the form of higher premiums. A premium is the amount a person pays for his or her health insurance each month.

One in three Americans had insurance through Medicaid or Medicare in 2016, and 9 percent were uninsured. Many can't get employer-paid insurance because they are either self-employed, work for a company that doesn't insure its workers, or have retired early. In some cases, they may be between jobs and their continued health coverage through COBRA (Consolidated Omnibus Budget Reconciliation Act) has run out. Passed in 1986, COBRA gives health coverage to workers and their families for limited periods under certain circumstances; for instance, in the case of job loss or a change in lifestyle or location as a result of death or divorce. The consumer with private insurance pays premiums; the amount varies widely according to gender, age, and geographic location.

Managed Care

Ever since the system began, employers have been trying to keep the costs of employee health care from increasing. For many years, the government tried, without great success, to regulate health-care costs. Finally, in 1973, the Health Maintenance Organization Act was passed. It gave grants and loans to those willing to start or expand a health-maintenance organization (HMO) that would benefit all members, charge the same monthly premium, and be set up as a nonprofit organization. It removed state restrictions if the HMO was certified by the federal government, and it required employers with twenty-five or more workers to offer an HMO option if requested. This last and most important provision, which expired in 1995, let HMOs into a market that had usually been closed to them. So-called managed care began to flourish.

HMOs started as a response to problems with the fee-for-service model. There was little if any monitoring of the number of medical visits, reasons for tests, costs of drugs, or length of hospital stays. Hospitals actually were paid by the day, so they had an incentive to encourage longer stays.

Managed care, the alternative system provided by HMOs, refers to various ways of financing and delivering health care. Basically, it is a way to contain costs by controlling services. Is this operation really necessary? Is there a more cost-effective way to manage the patient? In traditional medicine, the patient deals directly with the doctor, who generally decides on a treatment or orders tests without first considering how much they will cost. With managed care, the stated aim is the same—appropriate care for the patient—but the delivery is different. Expenses become a factor in providing care.

Managed-care organizations in the US health-care system today may differ in the details of how they are run, but they all operate with the same goal of delivering care while controlling costs. The most common of these are health-maintenance organizations (HMOs), preferred-provider organizations (PPOs), exclusive-provider organizations (EPOs), and point-of-service (POS) plans.

HMOs deliver health care through contracts with doctors, hospitals, and other medical personnel. The aim is health service at lower costs than traditional care. They try to do that by managing patient care and reducing expenses. The HMO member must usually choose a primary care physician (PCP), who acts as a so-called gatekeeper. (Some plans allow women to select an obstetrician/gynecologist as well as a PCP.) In many cases, a

PCP's referral is required to send the patient to a specialist—a way of limiting costs. In some plans, the patient may have to get a second opinion for a surgery. Not everything needs to be authorized by a PCP, however. Usually, a visit to an emergency room does not require a PCP's approval. Still, after a hospital visit, the patient may be transferred to a less-expensive facility or referred to home care to recuperate.

Kaiser Permanente, based in Oakland, California, is one of the nation's largest HMOs. It has nearly twelve million health-plan members in eight states and the District of Columbia, and it employs nearly 211,000 workers of all types and more than 22,000 doctors. It was founded in 1945 by industrialist Henry J. Kaiser and Dr. Sidney R. Garfield. The name comes from Permanente Creek, near Kaiser's first cement plant.

Kaiser Permanente, however, was not the nation's first HMO. Dr. Raymond G. Taylor created a temporary health-care system for the Los Angeles Board of Public Works that operated from 1908 to 1912. Baylor University in Texas started a hospital prepayment plan in 1929 to help ease the financial problems of the Great Depression. It was the first of several such plans that eventually joined to form the Blue Cross insurance network.

Kaiser Permanente's history actually began in 1933 when Kaiser and several other construction contractors formed a health-insurance network. Garfield got the contract to care for some five thousand workers. The Permanente Medical Group was reorganized in 1948 and acquired its present name in 1951. Over the years, the HMO constantly fought the opposition of the American Medical Association as well as various state and local medical societies.

Today, Kaiser Permanente is administered through eight regions. The Permanente Federation is a separate entity that focuses on making sure patient care and performance are standardized under one policy system. The ultimate governing body is a board of directors.

Those who manage Kaiser Permanente and other HMOs keep their eye on expenses through such methods as a utilization review. How many times did a patient see a doctor last month? How much did the HMO spend on the patient? The aim is to make sure the services are really necessary to give appropriate care. For those with chronic diseases such as diabetes, the HMO may designate a case manager for the patient to make sure the care providers don't overlap.

HMOs generally come in four models. In the staff model, doctors are salaried by the HMO. Their offices are usually in an HMO building, and in some cases they see only HMO patients. In the group model, the HMO has a contract with a physician group practice, which employs the doctors. If the group serves only HMO members, it is called a captive group model. If the group also treats non-HMO members, it is known as an independent group model. Since 1990, the network model has generally been the most often used by HMOs. In this form, the HMO can have a contract with groups, individual doctors, and independent practice associations. In the Independent Practice Association or open-panel model, doctors see both HMO and non-HMO patients.

Over the years, HMOs have come under a great deal of criticism. They have been the target of multiple lawsuits. A big complaint is that HMOs are more interested in making money for themselves than in the health of their clients. Many argue that, because of HMO restrictions, some patients are not given the care they need. An HMO is sometimes held responsible when a doctor it employs performs poorly. However, malpractice suits often fail because the HMO does not control the provided health care, but only the way it is financed. Other criticisms include that you can't choose your own doctor (in most cases); that the care is impersonal and operates like an assembly line; that patients have

Secretary of Health, Education, and Welfare Caspar Weinberger speaks about the Health Maintenance Organization Act, passed in 1973.

to give up their private health policies to join an HMO; and that there are often long waiting periods for health service delivery.

A PPO (preferred-provider organization) is a group of doctors, hospitals, and other health personnel. They join with an insurer to bring reduced-rate health care to the insurer's clients. A PPO offers many of the same services as an HMO, with a couple of significant differences. The monthly fees may be higher because it has greater flexibility. A member may see any doctor he or she chooses or go to any hospital. In an HMO, usually the member is restricted to the organization's list of hospitals. Employees are not always given a choice between an HMO and a PPO, but if they are, PPOs may be preferred because of their flexibility. Sometimes, however, HMOs may be the better deal if they offer more providers to the consumer.

Like HMOs, PPOs use a review system to make sure the provided health care is appropriate and within the cost limits. Usually, PPOs have a precertification requirement. For some outpatient surgery and for nonemergency hospital admissions, the insurer must give prior approval.

In the EPO (exclusive provider organization) setup, individual providers or groups of providers offer health care through written agreements with an insurer. The insurer reimburses the client only if the care comes from the designated network of providers. In turn, this network charges lower rates. The EPO and the network set fees for service. The EPO also helps to solve any problems that may occur between the network providers and the clients. EPOs can often offer lower rates than other managed-care facilities. However, they can also have strict limits, and an EPO member cannot go outside the network for care. Even in an emergency, the member may be charged if he or she uses a hospital outside the designated network. (For these reasons, EPOs have the fewest members of these types of health-care providers.) In contrast, a PPO member may be reimbursed for care received outside the designated-provider list.

The POS (point of service) plan has a little of both the HMO and the PPO. POS plans are sometimes called open-ended HMOs or PPOs. As in HMO and PPO plans, POS members may choose from a network of doctors and medical facilities. However, POS members have the option of being treated by doctors outside their network. If a member does so, the claim may not be entirely covered, as it would be if the care came from the plan's designated providers. If a POS member works within the network, however, all the paperwork is done for him or her, whereas if the member goes outside the POS network, he or she has to complete the paperwork. New POS clients choose their primary-care doctors from a list of preapproved physicians.

Medicare

The question of whether government should be involved in the provision of health care has been a central debate for decades. Yet, as Dr. Jerry Avorn writes in his book, *Powerful Medicines*, "The nation resolved the question of whether the government should get involved in medical care decades ago, with the passage of the first Pure Food and Drug Act in 1906 and of Medicare and Medicaid in 1965."

Initially, the Pure Food and Drug Act called for government inspection of meat products. It also stopped the manufacture and sale of poisonous medicines. The goal was mainly to ensure that products were correctly labeled. For example, it was at one time legal to buy and sell cocaine-based drugs as long as the label was correct. However, concerns eventually mounted about the safety of many products, for a variety of reasons. In one case, the government, backed by the Food and Drug Act, sued soft-drink manufacturer Coca-Cola. In the 1909 case, known as *United States v. Forty Barrels and Twenty Kegs of Coca-Cola*, the company was charged with putting too much caffeine in their product, which was thought to be harmful to children. The case dragged on for years with no one proving much of anything. Due to high costs associated with the lawsuit, however, Coca-Cola finally settled out of court in 1917.

Adverse publicity from the case led to two amendments to the Pure Food and Drug Act in 1912. Caffeine was added to the list of habit-forming and deleterious (harmful) substances that had to be shown on labels. The government was now definitively involved in health care.

The Medicare bill that President Lyndon B. Johnson signed in 1965 provides health insurance paid by the US government. After he signed the bill into law, Johnson handed the first Medicare card to former president Harry S. Truman, who was then eighty-one years old. The card, issued to all Medicare members, contains the member's name and Social Security number. It signifies that he or she is eligible for the medical benefits prescribed by the law. Members present the card at hospitals or other medical facilities when they seek treatment.

Medicare covers US citizens or those who have been permanent legal residents for five continuous years and are at least sixty-five years old. Some people are also covered if they are younger than sixty-five and have special, often devastating problems, such as disabilities, permanent kidney failure, or amyotrophic lateral sclerosis (ALS), commonly called Lou Gehrig's disease. Both Medicare and Medicaid are administered by the Centers for Medicare & Medicaid Services in the Department of Health and Human Services. They are financed by payroll taxes, the Federal Insurance Contributions Act, or FICA, and the Self-Employment Contributions Act of 1954.

Medicare originally had two parts: A, which covers hospital insurance, and B, for outpatient insurance. Part C, added later, called medical advantage, allows members with parts A and B to get health services through a Medicare private health plan. Medicare pays the plan a certain amount each month for each member. Members may have to pay a monthly premium in addition to the Medicare part B premium, and they may pay a fixed amount for each doctor visit. In 2006, part D was added to give seniors more prescription drug coverage.

Medicare has a number of regulations and restrictions regarding what is and is not covered. To qualify for Medicare coverage in the hospital or a skilled nursing facility, the patient must stay at least three times overnight. Nursing-home stays are covered if they provide skilled care (personal care such as cooking or cleaning is not covered) and if they follow a hospital stay. For instance, if a man breaks his leg and goes to the hospital, then goes to a skilled-care nursing home for rehabilitation, Medicare covers both costs.

A patient can stay in a skilled-nursing home for a maximum of one hundred days per ailment. In a hospital, the coverage is sixty days. That includes the room and meals, nursing services, lab tests, X-rays, operating-room costs, rehab services such as

Demonstrators rally in support of the Affordable Care Act in Montana in 2017. Montana expanded Medicaid under Obamacare that year.

occupational therapy, intensive care units, use of wheelchairs or other such equipment, and any drugs administered during the stay.

As of 2018, after sixty days in the hospital, the patient pays $335 a day from days sixty-one to ninety and the government pays the rest. If the patient is still in the hospital after day ninety, he or she can use a reserve fund. The patient pays $670 a day and the government pays the rest. Sixty days after the patient leaves the hospital or skilled nursing facility, he or she can return to either place and begin a new benefit period. If the patient can't afford the initial charge, Medicaid is called in.

Part B medical insurance helps to pay for some services that part A doesn't cover. It is a voluntary health-insurance plan with monthly premiums. It covers doctor and nursing services, X-rays and lab tests, some ambulance transport, chemotherapy, flu vaccinations and blood transfusions, and some outpatient treatments in a doctor's office. Also covered are such equipment as wheelchairs and walkers, oxygen for home use, eyeglasses for cataract surgery, and artificial limbs.

Medicare has many benefits, but it doesn't pay for everything. There are so-called gaps in coverage, such as hospital or skilled-nursing facility costs beyond certain day limits. To cover these gaps, some people opt for a medigap, or supplemental, insurance policy. These are health policies sold by private insurance companies. They help to pay for some of the costs that someone's original Medicare plan does not cover. There are ten standard medigap policies, and they must all follow state and federal laws. However, each plan may have different basic and extra benefits and each insurance company decides which medigap policy it will sell. It is therefore important for the prospective buyer to decide which gaps he or she needs to cover and to compare policies, because the costs of these policies vary. Those interested in a medigap policy can contact their local city or state health facility. In New York State, for instance, medigap buyers can call the Health Insurance Information, Counseling and Assistance program for help in deciding on the correct policy. It is costly and worthless to pay for a policy that doesn't cover what Medicare doesn't cover.

Medicare also usually doesn't apply outside the United States, meaning members are covered only if they are in the fifty states, the District of Columbia, Puerto Rico, the US Virgin Islands, Guam, American Samoa, and the Northern Mariana Islands. There are a few exceptions.

Medicaid

Like Medicare, Medicaid was created in 1965 and is funded by the federal government and the states. It is the country's largest funding source for those with limited income. Unlike Medicare, Medicaid is intended to serve primarily low-income citizens and legal residents, including the disabled and low-income families with children. Although the federal government provides broad program guidelines, each state sets its own rules for eligibility, benefits, and coverage. Each state determines what it considers to be low income. In Washington state, for example, a single person earning $1,397 or less per month is eligible for Medicaid. A four-person household earning less than $2,887 per month is also eligible.

Most but not all states set their income limits based on those of the Supplemental Security Income (SSI) program. Since 1974, this plan, administered by the Social Security Administration, gives monthly payments to elderly (sixty-five or older), blind, and disabled persons judged to be in need.

States generally determine Medicaid limits in one of two primary ways. Those considered "categorically needy" are eligible because they have a relatively low income and/or relatively low-value assets (houses, for instance, are considered assets). The "medically needy" category bases eligibility on income and assets plus medical costs. A person may have income and assets above the low-income limits but high medical costs that make him or her eligible for Medicaid.

Some people are eligible for both Medicare and Medicaid programs. Medicaid covers a greater range of services, such as paying for most long-term care both at home and in nursing facilities. Medicaid also pays many of the costs that Medicare doesn't cover in hospital and doctor bills.

Medicaid may go by different names in different states. For instance, it is called eMedNY in New York and Medi-Cal in California. States don't have to participate in the Medicaid program, but all have done so since Arizona joined in 1982. Some states use private health-insurance companies as subcontractors; others pay doctors and hospitals directly.

Although a person must have a limited income determined by each state to get Medicaid, even poverty doesn't mean he or she qualifies. There are many different requirements to be eligible for the service. There are special rules for disabled children at home, for those in nursing homes, for pregnant women with a family income below the poverty level, for those with disabilities, and for the elderly with low incomes.

A particular Medicaid plan, the Health Insurance Premium Payment (HIPP) program, operates in some states. HIPP may pay for private health insurance for a Medicaid user under specific circumstances. Suppose a person is on Medicaid or eligible for it and then health insurance becomes available through an employer. HIPP will decide if it is cheaper to use the employer's private plan or pay through Medicaid. This plan might be especially helpful to families with access to private insurance but who have children younger than nineteen who qualify for Medicaid. The entire family in this instance might be covered by HIPP. In California, the OA-HIPP program is specially designed to help adults with HIV/AIDS.

Mental Health Care

One in six American adults—or 44.7 million people—was living with mental illness in 2016, according to the National Institute of Mental Health. Yet only 43 percent of these individuals received mental health treatment.

Mental disorders fall into several major categories, including degrees of depression; bipolar disorder (extreme mood swings, once called manic-depression); schizophrenia (a brain disorder that might include hearing voices or feeling persecuted); anxiety and panic disorders; obsessive-compulsive behavior (including distressing thoughts and repetitive actions); and post-traumatic stress disorder (PTSD, severe fear or numbness following a terrifying experience such as war or rape). Other mental problems include agoraphobia (fear of traveling or leaving the home); eating disorders (from anorexia nervosa where a person doesn't eat to uncontrollable episodes of overeating); ADHD (attention deficit

Controlling Asthma Treatment Costs

Asthma is a chronic disease of the airways that causes wheezing and coughing and sometimes severe breathing problems. It affects some twenty-five million Americans, including 8.4 percent of children. Many of them rush to the emergency room for emergency measures when an attack occurs. This kind of ER use is costly. Programs aimed at reducing the disease can end up reducing ER costs as well.

Such a program, the Harlem Children's Zone Asthma Initiative, began in 2002. The program conducted a study of childhood asthma in Harlem, a largely African American section of the city. Because of present and historical systems of racial inequality and discrimination in the United States, African Americans are more likely to live in high-poverty neighborhoods, and asthma is often prevalent in poor areas.

The Harlem program tested children in a sixty-block area around the hospital. The discovered rate was five times above the national average. Parents and children were taught to manage their asthma by a combination of medicines and doctor or nurse visits. People were shown how to improve their environment by getting rid of mold, dust mites, or cigarette smoke.

The result was a drop from 35 percent to 8 percent of children who went to the ER or had an unscheduled doctor visit for treatment. Overnight hospital stays for treatment went from 8 percent to none over the same period. Experts say that this kind of program not only can help control the disease, it can cut the costs of treating it as well.

Asthma is a chronic but treatable condition—so long as those who suffer from it have access to health care.

hyperactivity disorder, a common mental disorder in children that affects the ability to function in school or other settings); autism (a brain disorder that impairs social interaction); substance-related disorders (misuse of alcohol or drugs); and Alzheimer's (a form of dementia usually affecting older adults). Treatment for many of these conditions can be expensive and lengthy—even lifelong.

Whether a person needs a psychologist or a psychiatrist depends upon the condition from which he or she is suffering. A psychologist studies all aspects of behavior and treats patients in hospitals, clinics, schools, and private practice. There are many different types of treatment, including clinical (the most common), which helps people cope with illnesses, injury, or severe crisis, and counseling, which provides help with everyday living. Clinical and counseling psychologists must have a doctoral degree, which requires five to seven years of graduate study. They must also complete an internship.

A psychiatrist is a medical doctor specializing in the diagnosis, treatment, and prevention of mental illness. As physicians, they can order a full range of laboratory and psychological tests in the treatment of patients and prescribe medication. Their education includes college and medical school. As new doctors, they spend the first year of residency training in a hospital and treating a wide range of mental illnesses. They spend at least three more years in a psychiatric residency where they learn to diagnose and treat these disorders.

Who pays for mental health treatment is another question entirely. Medicare patients are covered for mental health–care services in parts A through D. If a patient needs psychiatric care and goes to a Medicare-participating psychiatric hospital, part A covers 190 days. But that's it. Medicare will not pay any more for psychiatric care during the rest of a patient's lifetime. However, if the patient goes to a general hospital for a psychiatric problem, there is no 190-day limit.

More than 44 million Americans suffer from mental illness, yet less than half receive treatment, in part because of high costs.

Medicare provides outpatient services for the mentally ill, including diagnostic testing and office visits to monitor how well any prescribed drugs are working. Patients must pay coinsurance (a share of the cost of services after deductibles are paid) for psychotherapy services. Medicare also pays independent mental health providers such as psychologists, social workers, nurse specialists, and nurse practitioners. In January 2006, Medicare began paying for outpatient prescription drugs for mental illnesses under part D. Medicaid benefits also include long-term care for the mentally ill, and there is no waiting period for coverage. Anyone who meets the income and disability limits can qualify.

Medicaid also covers services for the mentally ill. The program covered 21 percent of US adults who had a mental illness in 2015, and 26 percent of adults with serious mental illnesses. Given that 14 percent of the total population is covered by Medicare, those with mental illness are more likely to be low-income or medically needy enough to qualify. Medicaid is also used to pay for treatment for people with substance abuse disorders, such as an addiction to alcohol or opioids. While having a substance abuse disorder does not help a person qualify for Medicaid, psychiatric or medication-assisted treatments for such disorders are covered on a more limited basis.

Chapter Three

REGULATING HEALTH CARE

Preventive medicine promotes overall health and seeks to preempt medical problems before they occur. Health-related regulatory agencies have much the same goal, with the added mission of protecting the public from dangerous substances. The Organization for Economic Cooperation and Development (OECD) reported that, in 2015, the United States had above-average rates of avoidable hospital admissions for asthma and chronic obstructive pulmonary disease (COPD)—261 per 100,000 people compared to an average of 237 across countries surveyed—and congestive heart failure (CHF)—347 per 100,000 people compared to an average of 228 across countries. "A high-performing primary care system," the OECD argues, "where

Opposite: An employee of the Centers for Disease Control and Prevention (CDC) is at work in her laboratory.

accessible and high quality services are provided, can reduce acute deterioration in people living with asthma, COPD, or CHF and reduce unnecessary admissions to hospital." Regulatory agencies working together with preventive medicine professionals, then, have a key role to play in improving a nation's overall health.

Centers for Disease Control and Prevention

The Department of Homeland Security protects US territory from terrorist threats and attacks and responds to natural disasters. Another government agency, the Centers for Disease Control and Prevention (CDC), might also be called a department of homeland security. Its mission is to protect US public health and safety.

The CDC is based in Atlanta, Georgia, and is part of the Department of Health and Human Services. It has ten other locations in the United States and its territories, including Alaska and Puerto Rico, as well as staff members in fifty states, 120 countries, local health agencies, and at various ports of entry. The CDC works with state health departments to keep the public informed about health decisions and potential epidemics such as the flu or the spread of diseases such as AIDS. It also notifies the public of workplace dangers such as asbestos contamination. In that case, the CDC would propose guidelines to assess the risk that workers face. The Occupational Safety and Health Administration (OSHA) would actually draft the proposed rule to be enforced. Both of these agencies work to improve US health overall.

In 1946, a World War II agency known as Malaria Control in War Areas became the basis for the CDC. It was called the Communicable Disease Center and was located in Atlanta. Malaria was then a problem in many of the southern US states. It is still a very common infectious disease worldwide. Malaria is transmitted by the female Anopheles mosquito and brings on a severe flu-like illness. At its worst, it can cause coma and death. In 2016, there were 445,000 deaths from malaria worldwide. In the first year of operation, CDC workers were mainly engaged in killing mosquitoes and used the insecticide DDT. At the time, the CDC staff was composed primarily of nonmedical personnel; they simply had to know how to drive trucks or use a shovel in the war against the mosquito.

In 1947, the CDC paid Emory University a token $10 price for the fifteen acres of land on which its headquarters are located today. (The land was actually paid for by Coca-Cola chairman Robert Woodruff, who had an interest in malaria control. He said mosquitoes were a problem when he went hunting.) From that beginning, the organization has become the country's main health promotion and prevention agency. Its staff, which numbered 369 in the first year of operation, now includes more than twelve thousand. They are engineers, scientists, economists, veterinarians, nurses, and physicians, to name just a few specialists.

Although it is still known by its original initials of CDC, the name-change in 1992 to Centers for Disease Control and Prevention reflects its increased role as the nation's health overseer. Because of its extensive work with communicable diseases, it is recognized as a world authority. It also has one of the few Biosafety Level 4 labs in the United States.

Biosafety Level 4 involves dangerous agents that can be fatal to humans such as the Ebola virus, smallpox (although there is a vaccine), or various exotic fevers. Only a handful of labs exist at this level in the United States. The staff has specific and thorough training in these types of agents. They wear hazmat suits (similar to spacesuits) and have self-contained oxygen supplies. At the lab entrance and exit, there are showers and ultraviolet light rooms to remove all traces of the materials. Doors are electronically secured, and access is strictly controlled by the lab director. These labs are entirely separated from the main facilities or they are in a controlled area that is isolated from all other building sites.

The CDC is also one of only two sites in the world designated by the World Health Organization (WHO), a United Nations agency created in 1948 concerned with worldwide public health, to hold stocks of the deadly smallpox virus. Smallpox was a human scourge for centuries. It is highly contagious. The victim comes down with chills, fever, nausea, and muscle aches. Then a rash appears that turns into pus-filled lesions. If the victim survives, the rash scars may be permanent. In the most severe form, the fatality rate is 50 percent among those who are not vaccinated.

The first smallpox epidemic recorded was in 1350 BCE and reached Europe around the fifth century CE. Since that time, millions of people have died of the disease. However, people began to realize that someone who survived smallpox was immune for the rest of his or her life. In the 1790s, English doctor Edward Jenner discovered the vaccination for smallpox. Over the years, the vaccine destroyed the disease so thoroughly that physicians in the United States stopped giving smallpox vaccines in 1972, except to military personnel, who it was thought might be sent to places where there was no vaccine. In 1979, WHO declared that the smallpox virus had been wiped out worldwide. The United States stopped vaccinating military personnel against the virus in 1990. Besides the CDC, the other official holder of the deadly virus is the Russian State Centre for Research on Virology and Biotechnology in Russia.

Food and Drug Administration

In addition to government facilities such as the CDC keeping watch on public health, there are regulatory bodies that do similar work. One is the Food and Drug Administration (FDA), an agency of the Department of Health and Human Services. The

FDA regulates food types, drugs, vaccines, dietary supplements, cosmetics, veterinary products, medical devices, and more. It also enforces section 361 of the Public Health Service Act, which deals with the spread of communicable diseases between states or between foreign countries and the United States.

The Food and Drug Act was signed by President Theodore Roosevelt in June 1906. Until that time, some federal and state laws tried to protect the public against the mislabeling of food products and other schemes. Among other things, the new act penalized the transportation of so-called adulterated food. That meant food that was colored to conceal damage or had fillers added to change the quality or strength. It also banned food and drug misbranding. The responsibility for carrying out these regulations went to the Bureau of Chemistry, headed by Harvey Washington Wiley. In 1927, the bureau became the Food, Drug, and Insecticide organization. In 1930, it was renamed again, this time called the Food and Drug Administration, or FDA.

By the early 1930s, it had became clear that food and drug safety laws were inadequate. However, it took the Elixir Sulfanilamide tragedy to push the US Congress into action. More than one hundred people in fifteen states died and many more became ill during September and October of 1937. They had taken a mixture that included sulfanilamide, a drug that in tablet or powder form was effective in curing throat infections.

The mixture had become deadly when Harold Watkins, chief chemist at S. E. Massengill Company in Bristol, Tennessee, discovered that sulfanilamide could be dissolved in diethylene glycol. The result was a mixture that tasted and smelled better than the original. Unbeknownst to Watkins, diethylene glycol was normally used as an antifreeze and is a poison. Soon shipments of Elixir Sulfanilamide were sent all over the country. At the time, there were no laws that tested new drugs to see if they were toxic, so no one tested Massengill's new concoction. The first shipments

Elixir Sulfanilamide killed more than one hundred people in 1937. It hadn't been properly tested because there were no laws requiring tests.

went out in September and the first deaths were reported in early October. Although many people died, the death toll would have been far higher were it not for the efforts of federal and state health agencies to track down the prescriptions. Watkins committed suicide while he was awaiting trial.

Out of that fatal experience came the Federal Food, Drug, and Cosmetic Act, signed by President Franklin D. Roosevelt in June 1938. It is the basis for FDA authority today. It forces a review of new drugs before they hit the market, bans false claims for drugs, and mandates factory inspections where drugs are made. It sets higher standards for food control, and it also covers cosmetic and therapeutic devices. According to FDA Consumer magazine, "25 years later, it saved the Nation from an even greater drug tragedy—a thalidomide disaster—like that in Germany and England."

In 1959, Tennessee senator Estes Kefauver headed a committee looking into pharmaceutical drug companies. It was learned that some of the companies gave experimental drug samples to doctors. The doctors then gave the untested drugs to patients and were paid for collecting the data on their reactions. Kefauver and the committee called for amendments to the Food, Drug, and Cosmetic Act. Their efforts were aided by the seriousness of the thalidomide disaster in 1961, mainly in England and Germany but also to some degree in Canada and the United States. Pregnant women had been given the sedative thalidomide to calm anxious nerves. The result was thousands of birth defects. Generally, the newborns were missing limbs or parts of limbs. The shocking pictures helped to pass the 1962 Kefauver-Harris amendment, also called the Drug Efficacy Amendment. Among other things, the law required informed consent of the consumer when testing experimental drugs. What's more, before the amendment, drug companies only had to show that their new products were safe. Now they had to show that the new drug was both safe and effective. However, many herbal and so-called natural medicines—those with no artificial ingredients—are exempt from FDA requirements.

The FDA has many branches that help do its work. The Center for Food Safety and Applied Nutrition is responsible for the safety and labeling of most food and cosmetic products. The Center for Drug Evaluation and Research sets requirements for new prescription drugs, generic drugs, and over-the-counter (nonprescription) drugs. The Center for Biologics Evaluation and

Thalidomide, Then and Now

The thalidomide disaster might have been far worse in the United States were it not for the stubbornness of an FDA medical officer. Frances Oldham Kelsey's first assignment when she joined the FDA in 1960 was to examine the data on thalidomide. She found the application data weak and inadequate. Kelsey insisted that the drug company, Richardson-Merrell, conduct further tests.

According to FDA historian John P. Swann, the tug-of-war between the drug company and Kelsey was fierce. "It's fascinating to see how many letters and communications went back and forth. She was asking for additional data, and what they were sending was in her eyes insufficient to answer the questions she was raising. She was increasingly pressured by the sponsor to get the drug approved. She didn't back down."

Because of her insistence, the drug company withdrew its application in March 1962, thus possibly saving many more infants from birth defects. For her work, President John F. Kennedy gave Kelsey the President's Award for Distinguished Federal Civilian Service.

After thalidomide was banned, researchers continued to conduct experiments with the drug. It is now in use under certain tightly controlled conditions. In 1998, the FDA approved it for treatment of a certain type of lesion under the brand name Thalomid. In 2006, the drug received FDA approval in some circumstances for patients with multiple myeloma, cancer of the body's plasma cells. According to a 2014 risk evaluation strategy from the manufacturing company, Celgene Corporation, if there is no other treatment available, women of childbearing age should have negative pregnancy tests before being prescribed the drug, with a new prescription required every four weeks.

Francis Oldham Kelsey, an FDA medical officer, probably saved many infants' lives when she insisted that thalidomide may be dangerous.

Research watches over blood, blood products, vaccines, and the like. The Center for Devices and Radiological Health approves all medical devices. The Center for Veterinary Medicine regulates food and drugs for animals, but not vaccines, which come under the US Department of Agriculture. Other branches include the National Center for Toxicological Research, the Office of Regulatory Affairs, and the Office of the Commissioner.

The FDA is the watchdog over many, many products that affect the health of Americans. Its authority is widespread, so much so that governmental and nongovernmental organizations keep an eye on the watchdog. Even so, the FDA gets its share of complaints and criticism. For instance, there were many complaints over the heparin mistake, reported by the *Washington Post* in early 2008. Its February 19 headline read: "FDA Says It Approved the Wrong Drug Plant." The confusion concerned the blood thinner heparin. Millions of people each year take the drug to prevent complications after surgery, among other uses. But by the end of 2007, there were hundreds of reports of bad reactions from heparin, such as breathing difficulties. Four people died. The FDA admitted its mistake. When the Chinese company that makes an ingredient for heparin applied for approval, the FDA thought it had already inspected the firm because it had inspected another factory with a similar name. It immediately sent a team of inspectors to China. Some in Congress believe that the FDA is not large enough to inspect the thousands of drugs and ingredients that are imported.

What kind of safety net does the FDA have for testing drugs? The three-phase process—although not without error, as seen in the heparin scandal—aims to be thorough and painstaking. However, as the FDA itself admits, no drug is absolutely safe. An adverse reaction is always a slight possibility.

Before phase 1 begins with a new drug, animal tests are performed. If the review board approves the results, the drug is then ready for clinical testing. This is the first time that the drug will be used on humans. The subjects are sometimes patients, but are more likely to be healthy volunteers, as many as eighty in a test. The study aims to answer these questions: How effective is the drug? Does it do what it's supposed to do? What are possible side effects?

If all of that goes well, it's on to phase 2. These tests are more detailed and involve more subjects. Can a patient with a specific condition be treated efficiently with this drug? Phase 3 may involve a few thousand people. The effects of the drug are studied in even greater detail.

This whole process can take a long time. The FDA says that testing of a new drug might take as long as eight years. This means that someone with a cancer diagnosis could die well before a promising new drug is available on the market. For a patient with a life-threatening disease, a drug not yet approved may be allowed under what is known as compassionate drug use. This refers to a terminally ill patient who is given an unapproved drug because no other is available. The FDA calls them investigational drugs, first approved in 1987 for the critically ill.

Compassionate drug use is under tight control. Patients who are not in clinical drug trials may get an unapproved drug either by the expanded access program (EAP) or by single access. For example, a drug company may offer a drug that is in phase 3 but is not yet approved for general use to those not in a clinical trial. The FDA might approve the use of the drug if the tests so far have been encouraging. For a patient not in a clinical trial or an EAP, his or her doctor may request its use from the company that is sponsoring the drug. If the company consents, both the drug company and the doctor work together to request permission for use from the FDA.

Genentech, a drug company in San Francisco, makes a drug called Avastin. It has been approved for the treatment of colon cancer and some lung cancers. But in February 2008, the FDA approved its use with chemotherapy for breast cancer patients. A study showed that the drug caused a reduction of more than 50 percent in the spread of the disease. This shortened time for FDA approval was allowed under the accelerated approval program. The accelerated program allows the FDA to sanction a drug for life-threatening diseases based not on final approval, but on positive clinical test results. According to the FDA, "approval of a drug based on such endpoints is given on the condition that post marketing clinical trials verify the anticipated clinical benefit."

Another Health Watchdog

A major group that keeps tabs on US health care is the Joint Commission, formerly the Joint Commission on Accreditation of Hospital Organizations. This private, not-for-profit organization was founded in 1951 and raises millions of dollars each year, mostly from the fees that it charges hospitals for letting them know whether or not they are complying with federal rules. An international branch, the Joint Commission International (JCI), was created in 1997. It surveys hospitals outside the United States.

The Joint Commission checks and officially recognizes (meaning it grants the legal credentials to) nearly twenty-one thousand health-care organizations, including general, children's, and rehabilitation hospitals, home health services, health-care networks, long-term care facilities, clinical laboratories, and ambulatory-care providers. It looks at a facility's performance in key areas, including whether or not patients receive the promised treatment and services. The Joint Commission employs hundreds of doctors, nurses, and other health-care professionals to conduct accreditation surveys. The surveyors do not assess the work of individual doctors.

After the Joint Commission surveys a hospital, it lets the hospital know its decision, but it does not open its findings to the general public. Even so, the surveyed hospitals all want to do well. If they are accredited, they are eligible for Medicare and Medicaid funds—a big incentive.

The Joint Commission, alongside federal regulatory agencies and laws, helps to ensure that health care in the United States, as well as drugs and treatments that might affect a person's health, achieve minimum standards of quality. In this way, many health problems are prevented, and overall health-care costs are lowered in the process.

Chapter Four

KEY CONTROVERSIES

The debate over health-care reform reached a frenzy when newly elected president Barack Obama instigated talks around what would eventually become the Patient Protection and Affordable Care Act, signed in 2010. Republicans attempted to repeal or undercut the law, nicknamed Obamacare, again and again to no avail. Their efforts were renewed after Republican Donald Trump was elected in 2016. Congress considered several proposals to repeal or replace Obamacare in 2017, all of which ultimately failed. However, Republicans did succeed in repealing the individual mandate, which requires that most Americans have health coverage. The move is expected to increase premiums by

Opposite: Congresspeople Jackie Speier and Barbara Lee participate in a 2017 press conference in support of the Affordable Care Act, which Congressional Republicans had threatened to repeal.

10 percent and result in thirteen million fewer insured Americans by 2027, the nonpartisan Congressional Budget Office reports.

So why are some groups so opposed to the Affordable Care Act or to the idea of universal health coverage in general, while others argue that it is necessary and a human right? Issues of inequity, inefficiency, and cost are all at play.

A Brief History of Health-Care Reform

Through the years, government leaders have attempted to improve the US health-care system. For instance, in 1964, President Lyndon Johnson's goals for his Great Society included health legislation. Medicare and Medicaid were enacted in 1965. However, the United States under President Johnson also became increasingly involved in the war in Vietnam. Health-care reform faded into the background.

In 1974, President Richard Nixon introduced the Comprehensive Health Insurance Act. It said that employers must buy health insurance for employees. It set up a federal health plan with payments based on income. Then, a break-in at Democratic National Committee headquarters at the Watergate complex in Washington, DC, led to the Watergate scandal. President Nixon was forced to resign in August 1974. His proposed health-care plan fell by the wayside.

Under the Bill Clinton administration in 1993, a health-care reform package was created by then–first lady Hillary Rodham Clinton. It proposed that all citizens had to be enrolled in a qualified health plan. Coverage and out-of-pocket expenses were detailed. Those below a certain income level paid nothing. However, Republicans and the insurance industry were major critics. They said that the plan restricted a patient's choice and that it was overly bureaucratic—meaning government was too involved.

The Health Insurance Association of America sponsored so-called Harry and Louise commercials, which were very effective. They showed a middle-class couple in despair over the complexity of the proposal. Democrats did not aid the Clinton effort either. Instead of uniting behind the president, many offered plans of their own. Democratic Senate Majority Leader George J. Mitchell introduced a compromise. Among other things, it made small businesses exempt from the proposal. No compromise among the various factions could be reached, and the Clinton health-reform plan was withdrawn in August 1994.

In 2006, the state of Massachusetts passed a universal health coverage law, setting the standard for a state-run health-care exchange upon which Obamacare would later be based. The reform was passed under the tutelage of then-governor Mitt Romney and helped insure more than 97 percent of Massachusetts residents. Obama openly pointed to "Romneycare" as a model for Obamacare, but as the Republican presidential candidate running against Obama in 2012, Romney would reject the idea that a similar law should have been implemented on a national scale, pointing to increased taxes and Medicare cuts associated with the Affordable Care Act. The Massachusetts exchange proved dysfunctional and was ultimately scrapped in favor of merging with HealthCare.gov, the federal enrollment site.

Health Insurance

To talk about health-care reform is to talk about money. It's a fact that health care costs money, and it's a fact that health-care costs are always on the rise. How is all this care to be paid for?

Any health plan centers around health insurance. Before the first medical insurance, patients had to pay all costs themselves. In 1911, the first employer-sponsored group disability policy was issued by the Equitable Life Assurance Society of New York. This group policy for Pantasote Leather Company of Passaic, New Jersey, granted insurance coverage to its 121 employees. Later, such policies would grow into modern health-insurance programs, into which people pay money a little at a time to ensure that they'll pay less when they need routine and emergency procedures.

In the 1920s, some hospitals began to offer treatment on a prepaid basis. Baylor College of Medicine in Waco, Texas, set up a health plan for teachers in 1929. For six dollars a year, teachers were guaranteed twenty-one days of hospital (inpatient) care.

Soon, similar plans emerged. The Hospital Service Association (now Blue Cross Blue Shield of Minnesota) first used a blue Greek cross as a symbol for the organization in 1934. The idea spread. The American Hospital Association in Chicago began to use the symbol of the blue cross in 1939. It was meant to signify an organization that would maintain high medical standards. The Blue Cross Association was founded in 1960.

The first Blue Shield plan was founded in Tacoma, Washington, in 1917. Monthly fees were paid to bureaus made up of doctors who provided medical care. The official Blue Shield plan was offered in California in 1939. Today, Blue Cross and/ or Blue Shield offer health insurance plans in all fifty US states. In most states, they also administer Medicare.

A health-insurance policy is a contract between an insurance company and the person who buys it. The contract details the kind of care given and what it costs. It can be renewed on a yearly or monthly basis. Several buyer obligations are specified. The premium is the amount the buyer pays each month for the service. The copayment, or copay for short, is the amount that the buyer must pay for a doctor's visit before the health plan kicks in. For example, the buyer might be charged a copayment of thirty-five dollars each time he or she visits the doctor. The deductible is the amount the buyer pays before the health plan begins to pay. The deductible might be a few thousand dollars a

The Hospital Service Association (today known as Blue Cross Blue Shield of Minnesota) was an early provider of health insurance in the United States.

year. Only after that amount is reached will the plan start to pay for medical services. Other obligations may include dollar limits on coverage or certain services that are excluded from the plan. With prescription drug plans, the buyer has to make a copayment, and the insurance company picks up the rest of the drug expenses.

Inefficient and Unfair?

Health care in the United States is often inefficient. It is certainly inefficient in its handling of the uninsured, a part of the population that places a great burden on the system. The system itself, which includes about six thousand US insurance companies, involves a vast number of people. It is bogged down not only in health-care costs, but in heavy administrative costs, such as employee salaries, paper supplies, and office machinery. In the insurance industry, general and administrative costs comprise more than 60 percent of expenses. When it comes to spending in US hospitals, administrative costs amounts to 25 percent of all expenses, compared to 16 percent in the United Kingdom and 12 percent in Canada.

In addition, US health care is the most heavily regulated industry in the country. Most of the cost comes from Food and Drug Administration regulations and medical malpractice. A charge of medical malpractice claims that the health-care provider (called the defendant) was negligent in his or her treatment of a patient (called the plaintiff). The defendant is usually a doctor, but he or she may be a therapist, nurse, or dentist. The plaintiff may be deceased, in which case the suit is brought on his or her behalf by the administrator of the estate. To win a malpractice case, the plaintiff must show that: (1) the defendant had a duty to perform, as is the case whenever a provider agrees to care for a patient; (2) the provider did not perform the standard of care, as judged by the testimony of experts or by an obvious error; (3) the provider caused an injury; and (4) there are damages to the patient—financial or emotional. Without damages, there can be no claim.

Most Americans with adequate insurance can receive the best health care in the world. Most have access to hospitals with up-to-date facilities and equipment. Most are within reach of skilled professionals, and can get care without delay. But not all. US health care is unfairly distributed. Those without adequate insurance or those who live in rural areas may not get to see qualified personnel. The system of government and private programs means that millions of Americans lack coverage. The uninsured may get treatment in the emergency room, but unless they are admitted to a hospital, they may receive little or no follow-up care.

Even among those who are insured, there are coverage gaps. A person who changes jobs might find that his or her new medical insurance doesn't kick in immediately. Someone may retire early and not yet be eligible for Medicare, which may mean missing a doctor's visit or not taking medication because it's too expensive. This results in a decrease in the nation's overall medical health and a greater drain on the system through ER visits and long-term care.

There are also inequities in health care for minorities in the United States. Many reports indicate that minorities get lower-quality care than do white Americans. What's more, long-term systemic racism has meant that minorities often live in higher-poverty neighborhoods, which are often underserved from a public health perspective, and higher incidence of certain illnesses is just one result. A landmark 2002 study by the Institute of Medicine, an independent research organization, said that even when racial and ethnic minorities have the same income and insurance, they often receive lower-quality health care. They are often less likely to be given appropriate heart medicines or undergo bypass surgery. They are less likely to be placed on the organ transplant list or receive kidney dialysis. They are more likely to get less-desirable procedures, such as a leg amputation for diabetes. Sometimes white doctors stereotype racial and minority patients, regarding them, for instance, as prone to drug abuse. Other times, white doctors just have difficulty relating to racial and minority patients and, therefore, have difficulty explaining medical procedures or problems.

This problem persists today, as the CDC reports a higher rate of obesity, infant mortality, asthma, breast cancer, and adult HIV infection in African Americans than in white Americans. A report by the US Department of Health and Human Services' Agency for Healthcare Research and Quality found that most disparities faced by Hispanics and African Americans had not changed significantly between 2000 and 2015. The report showed that

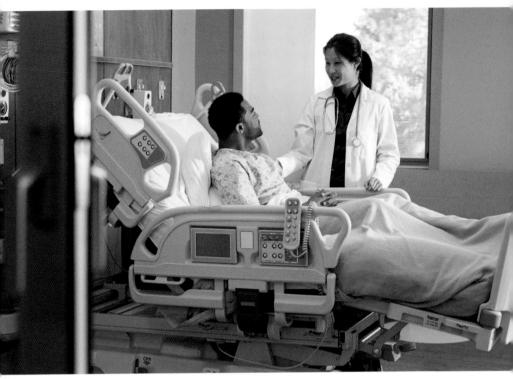

Minority patients often receive inferior health care compared to that of white patients because of widespread institutional racism.

poor, low-income, and even middle-income households receive worse care than high-income households.

Much of the problem of lower-quality health care is attributable to the fact that many minorities have less access to good care. African Americans, Hispanics, Native Americans, and Asian Americans are reportedly more likely to be treated by a doctor with less training than the average doctor. Doctors also often don't have a clear understanding of their patients' language or culture.

Racism affects health care. The stress of discrimination can directly affect a person's health, as can living in poor or unhealthy neighborhoods. People who live in poor neighborhoods may not have ready access to a pharmacy for medicines. They are less likely to go to a doctor, and even if they have insurance, they might not have money for medicines. They are more likely to go to work even when they are feeling ill because they may fear losing their jobs. People who live in a deteriorating neighborhood with boarded-up or abandoned buildings that collect dust and junk are more likely to suffer from asthma and other respiratory illnesses.

The Uninsured

About 9 percent of the American population has no health insurance. According to some studies, that is why a number of Americans die prematurely. While the figures vary widely and can be controversial, some claim that as many as forty-five thousand people per year die because they don't have health insurance. Other reports have found no correlation at all, but in the end, the effect of being without health insurance is quite difficult to gauge. In any case, many argue that some premature deaths must occur, given that the uninsured have access to fewer medical checkups, screenings, and procedures, and little or no preventive care. And the Agency for Healthcare Research and Quality reported in 2017 that uninsured people receive worse care than the privately insured.

Who are these people at risk and why aren't they covered? The likelihood of being uninsured in the United States is usually determined by such factors as income, age, parental and familial relationships, race, work and citizenship status, and company size.

Most of the uninsured in America are the working poor. They may be earning just enough to scrape by. If they are offered health insurance on the job, they may not be able to afford it. If they work part-time, their employer probably does not offer insurance. While the Affordable Care Act has required most Americans to

Strange Bedfellows?

A report from Dr. Claudia Henschke of Weill Cornell Medical College in New York City surprised the medical community. Her 2006 study concluded that the widespread use of CT scans could prevent as much as 80 percent of lung cancer deaths. (CT, or computed tomography, scans are X-rays enhanced by a computer to produce two-dimensional cross sections of the body's internal organs.)

However, an article in the New York Times in March 2008 cast a suspicion of bias on Henschke's study. It said that although the study claimed its funds came from a charity called the Foundation for Lung Cancer: Early Detection, Prevention & Treatment, "small print at the end of the study ... noted it had been financed in part" by Liggett, maker of several cigarette brands. Dr. Otis Brawley of the American Cancer Society called the Liggett funding "blood money." Henschke was also earning royalties from CT-machine companies.

It is rare for research studies to accept funds from cigarette makers for fear of undue influence. Although the results of the study seemed remarkable, critics cautioned that more studies were needed to make sure the findings were correct. In 2010, the *New York Times* reported that a large government-financed study found similar, though less dramatic results: a 20 percent reduction in former and current heavy smokers' risk of death from lung cancer as a result of annual CT scans. In any case, the cost of wide use of CTs to look for lung cancer would be extremely high, and such funds might be more effectively used in anti-smoking campaigns.

be insured, exemptions have been extended to those for whom health coverage is unaffordable, to citizens living abroad, and to other groups. People of color such as African Americans and Latinos were more likely to be uninsured in 2016, the Kaiser Family Foundation reported. One of the biggest obstacles that year was still cost, with 45 percent of uninsured adults saying coverage was just too expensive for them. Another 23 percent said that they were uninsured because they had changed employers or lost their jobs, while 12 percent said that they had lost their Medicaid coverage. Citizens comprise 78 percent of the uninsured population. Undocumented immigrants aren't eligible to purchase insurance in a marketplace or to receive Medicaid.

The Affordable Care Act also ensures that more young adults were insured by allowing them to stay on their parents' insurance longer, until the age of twenty-six. In the past, this group has been more likely than most to be uninsured. Financial guru Ray Martin offered these two reasons for the lack of insurance for this group: first, fewer jobs now have full benefits. Many consulting or freelance positions don't offer health benefits. Second, young workers often feel they don't want to pay thousands of dollars a year for benefits they don't yet need. Young and healthy for the most part, they can't yet imagine being sick.

Most of the uninsured do work. In fact, 75 percent of the nonelderly uninsured had one or more full-time workers in their family in 2016. However, they may have jobs that do not offer health coverage, or they may not take it when offered; most cite the high cost of insurance as the reason. They may also be part-time workers, where health insurance is not often an option.

The uninsured in the United States have increasingly become a focus of concern. After World War II and the rapid growth of the economy, most Americans had health insurance. Blue-collar workers had union contracts that guaranteed health benefits. White-collar workers were covered by their employers, with whom they generally stayed for long periods. People tended to join a company and stay there, perhaps for their entire working lives. However, that is less and less true today. In general, workers no longer spend a lifetime, or even many years, with the same company. In today's frequently changing market, workers average just about four years on the same job. Those in the technology field tend to change jobs more often than that. And with constantly rising health costs, some employers look for ways not to cover workers, especially those who may not stay for more than a few years. As a result, millions of Americans are uninsured. They can't afford to be.

Some workers find themselves in what, in insurance lingo, is known as the death spiral. A company sets up a cheap health plan for employees. Everyone may be healthy when they sign up, but as time goes on, people get sick. The cost to insure the unhealthy rises, as do the premiums. Healthy members may be able to find better plans elsewhere, which leaves the original plan with sicker people, and the premiums go even higher. The sick can't afford the coverage any longer, and eventually the company can no longer afford to offer health insurance, or must offer lower-quality plans.

Being uninsured in America often means doing without medical attention—another drain on the system. If a person with asthma can't pay for an inhaler, an attack may lead to the emergency room. Untreated diabetes may mean kidney failure or amputation. An untreated ear infection can cause hearing loss. Small health problems that go unchecked often result in major complications that are not only dangerous, but expensive.

What can uninsured Americans do when they need medical attention? Besides a trip to the emergency room, they cope in various ways. They may skip doses of their medications to make them last longer. They may know a doctor who gives free samples or even writes a prescription even though they aren't covered. Those living near the borders may go into Mexico or Canada to buy over-the-counter drugs that are prescription-only in the United States. However, the US government has cracked down on this border activity, making these sales much more difficult. Others may try to buy such drugs online.

The result is not only a hodgepodge of half-treatments, it is incredibly expensive. Medical costs have long been a major factor in cases of bankruptcy. However, according to *Consumer Reports*, bankruptcy filings dropped by 50 percent between 2010 and 2016, and most experts agree that more affordable health coverage as a result of the Affordable Care Act was a major factor.

Homeless and Uninsured

More than 550,000 people were homeless in the United States on any given night in 2017, according to the US Department of Housing and Urban Development. One in four lived in California, with experts citing the rise in housing costs as a primary factor. As the homeless population ages, too, California has seen "a dramatic rise in the number of people who die homeless. In Santa Clara County, the number of homeless deaths have more than doubled since 2011, with 132 people dying on the street last year," *Mother Jones* reported in 2017. A hepatitis A outbreak also contributed to rising mortality rates.

Many factors contribute to homelessness, including extreme poverty and a lack of affordable housing. The homeless population tends to suffer from serious health problems such as malnutrition and AIDS, as well as mental illness, diabetes, and alcoholism. Very few have health insurance of any sort, and fewer have the money to pay for care. As a result of where and how they live, the homeless generally go without treatment until the problem is so bad that it becomes urgent, which may lead to death or a trip to the emergency room. Everyone pays for the cost of this kind of medical attention.

In some big cities, where the homeless tend to congregate, clinics are set up to provide free health care. Since 1987, Health Care for the Homeless projects have been funded by the US Public Health Service. Beyond giving medical care, the projects work to find permanent jobs and shelter in an effort to get people out of homelessness.

Health Care in US Prisons

The United States houses more people behind bars than any other country in the world. Inmates of US jails and prisons number more than 2 million. China, with a far larger population, has about 1.6 million imprisoned. Many US inmates suffer from such ailments as hepatitis, tuberculosis, AIDS, substance abuse, and mental illness.

In the case of *Estelle v. Gamble* (1976), an inmate of a Texas prison charged the corrections department with cruel and unusual punishment for not treating a back injury he incurred during prison work. Other inmates may have complained in other prisons, but this time the case got to the US Supreme Court. Citing the Eighth Amendment, the Court ruled that prisoners have a constitutional right to health care. (The Eighth Amendment states: "Excessive bail shall not be required, nor excessive fines imposed, nor cruel and unusual punishments inflicted.")

In 2015, about one-fifth of prison expenditures in the United States went to health-care services—a total of $8.1 billion. Some states require prisoners to make a copayment, ranging from two to ten dollars, for some medical visits. The idea behind the plan is to cut down on unnecessary medical time off by inmates. However, if the prisoner does not have the money for the copay, he or she cannot be refused medical treatment.

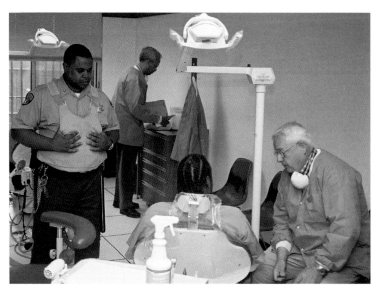

A dentist sees a patient at San Quentin State Prison in California. In 2005, a federal judge said health-care facilities there were horrifying.

Medical Underwriting

Medical underwriting was a process that insurers used to accept or reject those who applied for health or life insurance before the Affordable Care Act was passed. The idea was to keep premiums as low as possible. To do so, the insurer asked questions about any preexisting medical conditions and would often reject the applications of those with such conditions. Diseases such as arthritis or heart problems might make someone uninsurable, but so could being twenty-five pounds overweight. In some states, however, medical underwriting was illegal.

The Affordable Care Act made rejecting someone from health insurance coverage because of preexisting conditions illegal. Whether and how this popular provision of the controversial law should be preserved in some way should the Affordable Care

Act be repealed or replaced remains a key topic for debate. In 2016, the Kaiser Family Foundation estimated that 27 percent of adults in the US younger than sixty-five had conditions that might prevent them from getting health insurance coverage should medical underwriting become legal again.

The Anti-Patient-Dumping Law

In 1986, Congress passed the Emergency Medical Treatment and Active Labor Act (EMTALA). Some call it the law against patient-dumping. According to the American Academy of Emergency Medicine, EMTALA "requires hospital emergency departments (EDs) to provide any individual coming to their premises with a medical screening exam (MSE) to determine if an emergency condition or active pregnancy labor is present. If so, the hospital must supply either stabilization prior to transferring the patient or a certification (signed by the physician) that the transfer is appropriate and meets certain conditions."

EMTALA made it illegal for emergency rooms to refuse treatment to people because they cannot pay or have insufficient insurance. It also stopped the practice of discharging emergency patients because their treatment would cost too much. Only after the screening exam to determine the illness or injury can a patient be referred to a clinic or primary-care physician.

EMTALA applies to participating hospitals—those that accept payment under the Medicare program. That means most US hospitals, except Shriners Hospitals for Children, Indian Health Services, and military VA hospitals. Even though the law requires hospitals to admit patients for emergency treatment, EMTALA does not pay for this care. It places the financial burden on the hospitals and emergency physicians. Therefore, some argue that the law is straining an already overburdened system. A large percentage of ER treatment is not covered. When medical bills are not paid, the provider may transfer the costs to those who can pay, meaning those who do have insurance are paying for those who do not. Otherwise, the provider absorbs the loss. Sometimes this results in the closing of ERs, which overcrowds others nearby—another drain on the system.

Regulating health care remains a difficult task, especially as new circumstances and laws arise. With more than 50 percent of Americans approving of the Affordable Care Act in 2017 and 39 percent opposed, the law seemed to be gaining in popularity just as many lawmakers were arguing it was financially unsustainable and needed to be overhauled or even repealed. What a replacement bill might look like remained unclear as of mid-2018.

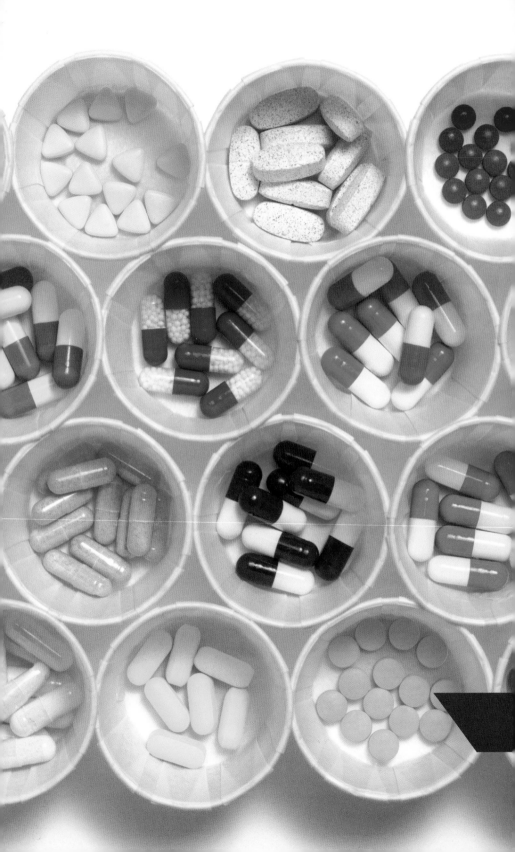

Chapter Five

PHARMACEUTICALS AND THE LAW

The United States spends more on prescription drugs—$1,011 per person in 2015—than any other country in the world. It may come as no surprise, then, that 14 percent of Americans in 2016 reported that they had, in the past year, decided not to fill a prescription because of the cost of that prescription. Such behavior is more common in the United States than in any of the other ten developed countries surveyed by the Commonwealth Fund, and it's even more common among uninsured Americans, more than 30 percent of whom have had to skip doses of their medicine for the same reason. Still, as expensive as prescription drugs are, they comprise only 10.1 percent of health care expenditures in the United States as a whole, according to the CDC.

Opposite: Americans spend more per person on prescription drugs than any other country in the world.

The high cost of prescription drugs has provoked considerable debate. The Commonwealth Fund argues that policies like universal health coverage and price control strategies such as centralized price negotiations might help reduce costs. However, the contingent opposed to universal health coverage argues that it will raise taxes and insurance premiums, ultimately making the financial burden on American consumers worse. Compounding debates around prescription drugs is the increasingly widespread abuse of such drugs, which can not only lead to addiction but increase crime rates.

The Pharmaceutical Industry

Pharmaceutical (drug) companies are in the business of researching, developing, advertising, and selling drugs. Most basic research on development is done at the National Institutes of Health (NIH) or at universities. A "new drug" advertised by drug companies is often an older medicine in a different formulation; for instance, it can now be used once a day instead of two or three times. By making changes to a drug's formulation, pharmaceutical companies can obtain a new patent for that drug, and ensure that no one else can sell it for a specific period of time. This lack of competition drives up costs for new drugs.

These companies are very successful. Prescription drug spending is expected to reach $610 billion by 2021. Drug companies are also very influential because of the nature of their product. Selling prescription drugs is not like selling dishwashers or bicycles, which people can live without. In many cases, people cannot live without the drugs that keep them healthy or free of pain. That fact gives drug industries a lot of power. It also makes them subject to a lot of criticism.

Pharmacists and drugstores have been around for centuries. Major pharmaceutical companies emerged in Europe and the

United States in the early twentieth century, aided by the discovery of such drugs as penicillin. Before penicillin, it was not uncommon for people to die from infections that resulted from a mere scratch.

The real growth of the pharmaceutical companies started in the 1950s. The structure of genetic material was discovered, and the DNA era dawned. In 1950, Mayo Clinic researcher Edward Kendall discovered the drug cortisone to treat arthritis and won the Nobel Prize for medicine. In 1955, Jonas Salk announced a vaccine to end the dreaded polio epidemics, which had crippled so many children and adults for so many years. New instruments and new medical techniques aided in the discovery of new drugs to cure human illnesses.

Drug use became more common in the 1960s, when major tranquilizers and antianxiety pills came on the scene. These compounds ushered in the so-called drug era. Wallace and Wyeth labs marketed meprobamate, known commercially as Miltown and Equanil. The drug was supposed to make you happier, less depressed, a better worker … a better everything. Miltown became so popular as a cure-all that Milton Berle, perhaps the most-watched TV comic of the time, called himself Miltown Berle. It was estimated that within a year, about 5 percent of Americans were taking Miltown. In 1966, rock band the Rolling Stones even sang about the drug and its calming influence on mothers dealing with their children.

Unfortunately, no one talked about Miltown's side effects. It was later found that the cure-all drug could become addictive as well as dangerous if taken with other drugs.

Still, the popularity of these antianxiety medications was nothing compared to one of the biggest-selling pharmaceutical drugs in history. Marketed by Hoffman–La Roche, this drug is called Valium. Until the late 1980s, when Xanax appeared, some sixty million Americans took Valium each year. It, too, turned out to be addictive.

The Pharmaceutical Top Ten

Ranked by prescription sales, these are the world's top ten pharmaceutical companies. Research and development (R&D) expenditures are also included.

Rank	Company	Headquarters	2016 Rx Sales (USD, in millions)	2016 R&D Spending (USD, in millions)
1	Pfizer	New York, NY	$45,906	$7,801
2	Novartis	Basel, Switzerland	$41,554	$7,916
3	Roche	Basel, Switzerland	$39,552	$8,717
4	Merck & Co.	Kenilworth, NJ	$35,563	$9,760
5	Sanofi	Paris, France	$34,174	$5,722
6	Johnson & Johnson	New Brunswick, NJ	$31,671	$6,967
7	Gilead Sciences	Foster City, CA	$29,992	$3,925
8	GlaxoSmithKline	Brentford, England	$27,775	$4,696
9	AbbVie	North Chicago, IL	$25,299	$4,152
10	Amgen	Thousand Oaks, CA	$21,892	$3,755

Prescription Drugs: A Political Issue

Many people find several reasons to complain about the US health-care system. Health insurance is too expensive. It doesn't cover everybody. With some plans, you can't choose your own doctor. It doesn't treat everyone the same. The rich get better treatment. And the list goes on. However, if there is one major issue about the system that everyone can agree on, it is that prescription drugs cost too much money. Low-income families may not be able to afford asthma medicines for their children. Retired people may suffer without pills for arthritis pain or skimp on diabetes medications because they cost too much. And, in a strange quirk of the system, those who need drugs the most and can afford them the least often have to pay higher prices for them. That's because people on Medicare who don't have supplementary insurance, such as AARP, are charged higher prices by the drug industry than, say, preferred organizations such as the Veterans Administration (VA). That's because the VA can buy in bulk. The average insurance owner simply doesn't have any bargaining clout.

Drug companies are a powerful lobby in Washington, DC. Pharmaceutical companies have spent nearly $2.5 billion on lobbying in the last decade, and the vast majority of Congress members has taken campaign contributions from them—all but three senators and nine out of ten House of Representative members.

The job of lobbyists is to promote the interests of their companies. That job is often made easier by their connections. For instance, since 2000, fifty-six or more former justice and Drug Enforcement Administration (DEA) officials have gone to work in the pharmaceutical industry. One might well assume that they maintain a sympathetic ear in the government. Drug companies also contribute handsomely to political campaigns. For instance, they gave more than $2.4 million to Hillary Clinton's presidential campaign and $343,165 to Donald Trump's campaign in 2016. All this influence works. The drug industry has been successful in stopping imports of cheaper medicines from Canada and other countries. They won coverage for prescription drugs under Medicare in 2003. That stopped Medicare from using its huge purchasing power to bargain for low prices.

Today, the United States faces a prescription opioid epidemic. Many people are becoming addicted to pain medication, and two hundred thousand have died. As the *Washington Post* points out, that's "more than three times the number of US military deaths in the Vietnam War." Yet between 2014 and 2016, the pharmaceutical industry spent $102 million on Congressional lobbying, in part to ensure the April 2016 passage of a bill that makes it harder for the DEA to seize questionable shipments of narcotics from drug distributors. Many distributors had been making billions of dollars by selling pills under suspicious circumstances, and the DEA had been trying to crack down on such sales for years. A spokesman for a drug distributor argued that the bill, called the Ensuring Patient Access and Effective Drug Enforcement Act, didn't decrease enforcement but increased effective communication between all parties involved. However, former DEA official Joseph T. Rannazzisi commented, "The drug industry, the manufacturers, wholesalers, distributors and chain drugstores, have an influence over Congress that has never been seen before."

Drug companies want deep connections within the government because they are so dependent on federal decisions. The government buys massive quantities of drugs via programs such as Medicaid and the Veterans Administration. It is also the government that decides what drugs can go on the market and how they can be labeled.

In 2017, a man apparently under the influence of drugs rests in the Bronx, a neighborhood of New York City experiencing a drug epidemic.

Because of the industry's power and the products it sells, there are more and more calls for reform. In her book, *The Truth About the Drug Companies*, Dr. Marcia Angell, former editor-in-chief of the New England Journal of Medicine, argues that the FDA should be made stronger. She says that government regulations have weakened the FDA as a watchdog over the drug companies. She also believes that drug companies should not be in charge of the clinical testing of their own drugs. Instead, such testing should be supervised by a separate institute, perhaps within the National Institutes of Health.

Abuse of Prescription Drugs

Prescription drug abuse is on the rise, and young adults are among those most likely to use these addictive substances without a proper prescription. Those between ages eighteen and twenty-five are most likely to report nonmedical use of prescription drugs.

They are even commonly abused among secondary school students. In 2017, 5.5 percent of twelfth-graders had misused Adderall (a medication for attention deficit hyperactivity disorder, or ADHD) in the last year, 4.7 percent tranquilizers, 4.2 percent non-heroin opioids, and 3.2 percent cough or cold medicine.

Opioid use is growing more common in the United States. Opioids contain the same primary ingredient, opium, that is used in heroin, a highly addictive, dangerous, and illegal drug. Between 2000 and 2012, opioid-related hospitalizations in the United States increased 72 percent. More than 115 Americans die every day from an opioid overdose. What's more, the economic impact of such abuse is huge: $78.5 billion in health care, addiction treatment, criminal prosecution, and lost productivity every year.

Many teens think that if a drug has been prescribed by a doctor, perhaps to kill the pain of a knee injury, it must be okay for other uses—like getting high. The truth is that drugs taken without a specific prescription or used for other than the stated purpose can be just as dangerous as cocaine or any other narcotic. They can also be just as addictive.

Prescription drugs are vital, necessary, and generally safe when they are taken as directed. They help to ease depression. They treat ADHD. They deaden the pain of a football injury. However, if these same drugs are taken by someone who isn't depressed, doesn't have ADHD, or isn't injured, they can become dangerous to the person using them. A doctor who writes a prescription has presumably examined the patient and tried to rule out a bad reaction or allergy to the drug. The patient may also have been warned to avoid such activities as drinking alcohol or taking another drug while on the medication. The use of a drug outside the purpose for which it was prescribed is called abuse.

Prescription drug abuse is not only as dangerous as abusing street drugs, it's also just as illegal. Those who take a drug without a prescription or share a prescription drug with friends are breaking the law.

Why do people abuse prescription drugs? Besides the fact that some wrongly believe them to be safe, the truth is, they're available. Usually they sit right on the shelf of the family medicine cabinet, and who keeps track? Raiding the medicine cabinet is easier than arranging a cocaine purchase. Three types of prescription drugs are commonly abused: depressants, opiates, and stimulants. Central nervous system depressants reduce tension and anxiety and improve sleep. They work by slowing down brain activity, which makes a person calm or drowsy. There are two types of depressants: barbiturates, such as pentobarbital sodium (Nembutal), and benzodiazepines, such as diazepam (Valium). Opiates such as meperidine (Demerol) are prescribed for pain. They attach to receptors in the brain and spinal cord and stop pain signals from reaching the brain. Stimulants are used in the treatment of ADHD and depression. Such drugs as methylphenidate (Ritalin) boost brain activity, which results in more energy and alertness.

There is danger in taking any of these drugs without a prescription. Too many stimulants can cause an irregular heartbeat. Depressants mixed with other drugs can slow the heart so much that it stops. Even if there are no apparent side effects, prescription drug abuse leads to the same result as street drug abuse: addiction. This means the user craves this particular drug or substance. It can change his or her mood, outlook, weight, and certainly his or her life. Here's a simple-but-smart rule to follow: a person should never, ever take any prescription drug that hasn't been prescribed just for him or her.

Everyone has a role to play in keeping prescription drugs from being abused or trafficked illegally. Lawmakers, pharmaceutical companies, and individuals alike must work together if they want to prevent these drugs from driving up health-care costs and endangering lives.

Chapter Six

HEALTH CARE AROUND THE WORLD

Americans are decidedly split on the issue of whether they have the best health-care system in the world, or one that falls far short in comparison with other countries' programs. One thing is certain: the United States' health-care model is not the only one out there, and there is a lot to be learned from studying how other programs have succeeded and failed.

Government programs that give all citizens free or subsidized access to health care are known as universal health-care programs. Most of the cost is paid with taxes, compulsory health insurance, or a combination of both. Some patients may pay for parts of their care directly. Most developed and many developing nations provide

Opposite: The World Health Organization (WHO) is a United Nations agency concerned with worldwide public health. Its headquarters, shown here, are in Geneva, Switzerland.

universal health coverage to their citizens. The United States does not, although the Patient Protection and Affordable Care Act of 2010 sought to take a step in this direction. How successful are other nations' health-care systems? What are the drawbacks? Can any of these methods be applied to improving the US system?

The Commonwealth Fund is a private foundation that, according to its website, "aims to promote a high performing health care system that achieves better access, improved quality, and greater efficiency, particularly for society's most vulnerable, including low-income people, the uninsured, minority Americans, young children, and elderly adults." A 2017 report from the fund ranks eleven wealthy nations on the quality of their health-care systems according to five metrics: care process, access, equity, administrative efficiency, and outcomes. Here is the full ranking:

1. United Kingdom
2. Australia
3. Netherlands
4. New Zealand
5. Norway (TIE)
6. Sweden
7. Switzerland (TIE)
8. Germany
9. Canada
10. France
11. United States

Let's take a look at the health-care systems in some of these countries, and in other countries with notable or unusual models.

Canada

Public funds pay for Canada's health system and private facilities provide the services. Canadians took some steps toward universal care in the early twentieth century. However, various attempts to set up a nationwide system failed. Finally, in 1946, Saskatchewan passed the Saskatchewan Hospitalization Act. The province had suffered from a shortage of medical aid for many years, even creating a program in which a town could pay a doctor to practice there. The 1946 law gave free hospital care to most of Saskatchewan's citizens. Alberta province followed with a similar plan in 1950. Seven years later, the federal government passed the Hospital Insurance and Diagnostic Services (HIDS) Act. It paid half the cost of health programs in the ten provinces and three territories that make up the nation of Canada.

Universal health coverage actually began in 1966 with the Medical Care Act. It allowed each province to set up a universal plan, and it established the Medicare system. In 1984, the Canada Health Act was passed, putting an end to user fees and extra billing by doctors. There are many variations across the country concerning home and long-term care and prescription drugs.

Today, 90 percent of Canadians feel that eliminating the country's health-care system, called Medicaid, would constitute a fundamental change in the nature of their country. Some US politicians such as Vermont senator Bernie Sanders have touted it as a model to follow. Canadians don't pay copayments for doctor and hospital visits, though most have some supplemental insurance in addition to Medicare to help them pay for dentistry, prescription drugs, and other expenses. The federal government pays direct health-care costs for military personnel and for prison inmates. It also assumes responsibility for First Nations. These are native peoples, most of whom use the regular hospitals, although some are served by clinics on reservations.

Canada spends about 10 percent of its gross domestic product (GDP) on health care, as opposed to about 18 percent in the United States. Drug prices in Canada are lower, although they have been rising in recent years.

Magnetic Resonance Imaging

The MRI is a diagnostic tool that has been in use since the 1980s. Similar to an X-ray, it can take pictures of almost all tissues (instead of bones) in the human body. The patient lies inside a large magnet that is shaped like a cylinder. As the patient passes through the cylinder,

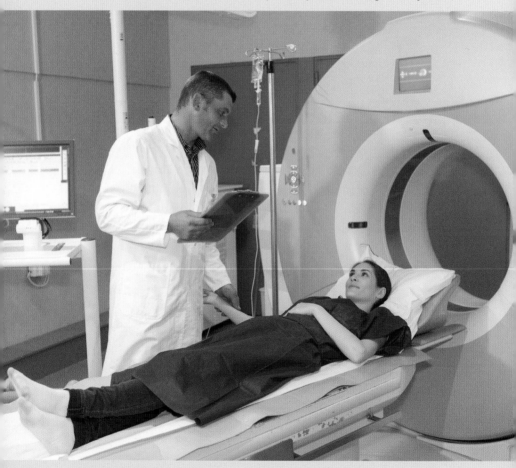

A doctor prepares a patient before using an MRI machine, which can take images of the entire human body.

strong radio waves are sent through the body. They go back and forth and make radio waves of their own. The radio waves become pictures that show any problems, such as tumors. The MRI does not expose the patient to X-rays or other radiation, and it is painless. (The radiation effects of X-rays can cause damage to living tissue, such as tissue in the bones called bone marrow.) Many patients, however, report feelings of claustrophobia inside the cylinder. For them, some facilities offer the open MRI, in which there is more open space around the body.

Having an MRI done is a costly procedure, and it's getting more expensive even for those who have insurance. In a September 2016 survey, more than 50 percent of workers reported having to pay $1,000 out-of-pocket for an MRI even though they had insurance—a higher percentage than ever before. However, as it turns out, MRIs can cost a lot more (or less) depending on where you have them done. Hospitals are more expensive than freestanding imaging centers, and some states are more expensive than others. The median network rate for a limb MRI at an Alaska hospital is nearly $4,000—or less than $1,000 in a freestanding facility. In California, there's a $1,000 difference. It seems that with MRIs, as with clothing and cars, it pays to shop around.

The system is far from perfect, however, as a new group of commentaries and studies published in British journal the *Lancet* concluded in February 2018. Waiting times for nonemergency procedures, imaging, and even surgeries are long. What's more, Canada is the only developed country that has universal health coverage that fails to also cover prescription drug costs. As a result, one in four Canadian households report having to skip or stop taking medications because they couldn't afford them. Meanwhile, Canada's indigenous population is suffering. This group, comprising 1.7 million people, has a life expectancy up to fifteen years shorter than non-Native Canadians do. They have tuberculosis at a rate that's 270 times higher and are more likely to suffer infant mortality and chronic disease.

The cost of health care for the average family has increased nearly 70 percent in the last twenty years, and Canada also has a shortage of doctors. To correct these complaints, the government made plans to train more physicians and to make it easier for foreign doctors to practice in Canada. However, in spite of record numbers of graduates from Canadian medical schools in 2017, doctors were still hard to come by in provinces like British Columbia. Like the United States, the country also faces swiftly rising prescription drug prices and a population that lives longer and therefore uses the health-care system for longer periods.

Costa Rica

The Republic of Costa Rica is about the size of the state of West Virginia. It has universal health coverage and one of the best health systems in Latin America. It also has the usual red tape and long waits. However, citizens have access to private health care that is high quality and affordable.

Health care is paid for by the government. The *Caja Costarricense de Seguro Social* (CCSS, the Costa Rican social security system) is responsible for providing low-cost care across thirty hospitals, about five hundred clinics, and around a thousand small attention units with basic capabilities. Affordable health care extends to noncitizens as well. Foreigners who live there pay a small monthly fee, based on income, to join the CCSS, or they buy insurance from the state. Doctors often work for the CCSS in the mornings and operate clinics in the afternoons and evenings.

Two first-class, ultramodern private hospitals, Clínica Bíblica and Clínica Católica, are affiliated with hospitals in the United States. Their charges are higher than public facilities but lower than any such US facility. Medical tourism to Costa Rica has become more popular, as travelers seek medical procedures there that are more affordable than in their own countries.

Cuba

The island of Cuba has a long history of medical care, with the first surgical clinic established in 1823. With the revision of the Cuban constitution in 1976, all citizens have the right to health care. Near-universal vaccinations were started in the 1960s, and many contagious diseases have been eradicated or greatly reduced. In 1970, a program was initiated to reduce the infant mortality rate. In 2007, Cuba announced it would start to computerize and create national networks in blood banks and medical imaging.

Cuba also started a program of training doctors, inviting many students from other Caribbean countries, Latin America, African and Middle Eastern countries, and even a few from the United States. The graduates are asked to return to their home countries and work in poorly served areas for a period of time as their medical education payment.

Following the end of Soviet subsidies in the 1990s, and as a result of the continuing US trade embargo, Cuba's medical care experienced shortages of supplies. Difficulty in obtaining certain medicines or treatments on the island has led, over time, to an increasing role of the black market in providing health care. There have been reports of patients being charged "under the table" for quicker or better service.

Life expectancy in Cuba is comparable to that of the United States, at just a fraction of the cost—$813 per person compared to more than $9,000 in the United States. The downside, though, is that low wages have held the medical sector and the economy back. As Fernando Ravsberg wrote in the *Havana Times* in 2018, "the reality is that if wages of medical personnel don't increase, the wages of cleaning staff can't get any better either. Patients will continue to receive 'stem-cell' therapy for free while they continue to slip and fall in puddles of water that nobody is cleaning up."

France

The World Health Organization has, in the past, ranked health care in the French Republic as the best in the world. The system's success is seen in the high life-expectancy rate of eighty-two years. Everyone who is salaried is covered by the national health plan known as *sécurité sociale* (social security). That includes spouses and children of the workers. Those who are not workers take out special coverage, called *l'assurance personnelle* (personal, or individual, insurance). In 2000, the government passed the CMU (*couverture maladie universelle*, or universal medical coverage) plan, covering those who have been residents for at least three months. The CMU plan was replaced in 2016 with the *protection universelle maladie* system, a similar approach with a different pay structure with respect to spouses.

French citizens can choose from a variety of doctors, specialists, and hospitals, regardless of patient income. But all of this service comes at a high cost. The French system is among the most expensive in the world. It takes up 12 percent of the GDP. High costs are blamed on overuse of prescription drugs and waste within the system itself. Even so, most citizens approve of their health services. They boast that waiting lines for surgery do not exist in France as they do in other nations with universal health coverage.

Germany

All 82 million citizens of the Federal Republic of Germany are covered by health-care plans. Until the age of sixty-five, they must pay into health insurance plans that are state-regulated or private. About 85 percent of the population has social health insurance and about 10 percent has private. Anyone earning less than $5,422 in US dollars each month is covered by social health insurance free of charge. Payments stop after retirement age but coverage continues until death. The German system boasts that waiting times for health services are rare, although there may be some minor delays for nonemergency surgery.

Despite its record, health care in Germany is not without its critics. Malpractice suits have increased over the past several years. The government has put strict limits on hospital expenses. Some fear this may cause hospital workers to leave the country for more lucrative jobs. Ambulatory services could be improved, and there are few facilities in the country for breast cancer screening.

Great Britain

The National Health Service (NHS) has been in operation in the United Kingdom since 1948. Every UK resident is covered by a system funded only through income tax and run by the Department of Health. It is the world's largest health service and one of the largest employers in the world, with a staff of 1.6 million and more than fourteen hundred hospitals.

Demonstrators in Middlesbrough, UK, show their solidarity with the National Health Service (NHS) in 2018.

Health Care: Universal Right or Personal Responsibility?

About 11 percent of Great Britain's population uses private health care, which is paid for by insurance or when people use the services. There are, however, several hundred private hospitals in Great Britain funded by private groups. They are licensed by the local health-care officials but not regulated by the inspectors who monitor NHS facilities. Private funds also supply some services within the NHS.

The NHS is unique among European systems in two ways. It pays directly for health expenses, and it employs nearly all the hospital doctors and nurses in England. Primary doctors, dentists, and other providers are usually self-employed and have contracts with the NHS.

For all its rules and regulations, the NHS has long been the target of criticism. Since the NHS offers free coverage to almost every citizen, it must sometimes ration its services. A heart attack victim takes priority over someone waiting to have a benign cyst (noncancerous growth) removed. As in many universal systems around the world, a major complaint is waiting time. And wait people do, sometimes for months. In response to criticism, the NHS has said it aims to make all waiting times no more than eighteen weeks. Another problem not unique to the British system is the rising cost of medical care and prescription drugs. Taxpayers who buy private health-care insurance argue that they are paying twice since they still contribute to NHS through their taxes. That criticism, however, is always present when there are existing public and private funds for services.

The Health and Social Care Act of 2012 constituted the largest reorganization that the NHS had yet seen. The goal was to tackle an aging population, more chronic conditions, and lagging survival rates for cancer and other ailments—all while dealing with funding concerns. The new law placed an emphasis on public health and encouraged clinicians to claim more freedom in the way they provide service. By 2017, however, many were reporting that the act had failed in improving services and reducing hospital admissions.

Iran

The Islamic Republic of Iran, a densely populated country in the Middle East, has about seventy-one million people. According to its constitution, Iranians are entitled to basic health-care services. The Ministry of Health and Medical Education operates general hospitals, as well as specialty hospitals for those with higher incomes. Public clinics serve those with limited funds. Iran's system has been ranked more efficient than the US health-care system, and overall health metrics in the country have improved over the last few decades.

Since the revolution of 1979, most Iranians have some access to health care. There have been many advances in medical technology. However, health services continue to be scarce in the rural areas. Communicable diseases such as cholera remain a problem, mostly because there are few facilities for treating wastewater in the country. In the capital city of Tehran, for example, in many areas raw sewage goes right into the groundwater. As Iran's population increases, so do the health risks because of this water pollution problem. Life expectancy is seventy-five years.

Japan

Japan's universal care requires coverage by either National Health Insurance or Employees' Health Insurance. National Health covers those who are self-employed or not employed, such as retired persons, students, expectant mothers, or workers in the fishing, forestry, or agriculture industries. Coverage includes illness or injury, dental services, and death of the insured or dependents.

Not covered are cosmetic surgeries, abortions, injuries resulting from intoxication, and medical services taken outside the country.

Employees' Health Insurance covers workers in medium and large companies, in government, and private schools. A separate plan takes care of small businesses. A program that covers the elderly—those over seventy—is funded by both plans.

Efficient as it is, Japan's system suffers from many of the ills of other industrialized countries. It is increasingly expensive. For instance, hospital stays in Japan are generally three times longer than in Western countries. As a result, Japan needs many more hospital beds, which are costly. Medical experts warn of other problems for health care in Japan, mainly that elderly retirees will soon outnumber young working citizens—especially given the exceptionally long life expectancy in Japan. How can that smaller number support so many older citizens?

Russia

The Russian Federation, or Russia, is the largest of the states that once formed the Soviet Union (USSR). In a 2016 *Bloomberg* report on the efficiency of national health care in fifty-five developed nations, Russia placed last. Just 2 percent of Russians express pride in their state health-care system, and 17,500 towns around Russia lack medical infrastructure.

Under Joseph Stalin, in office from 1927 to 1953, the Russian system of socialized medicine promised free health care to all citizens. The USSR (Union of Soviet Socialist Republics) was established in 1921 and lasted until 1992. It was the world's largest country, covering more than 8 million square miles (20.7 million sq km) and including fourteen separate republics in addition to Russia itself. By the 1980s, people in all the republics were covered by local and work-site clinics around the vast union. Large hospital complexes were available to most. This huge, multilevel operation

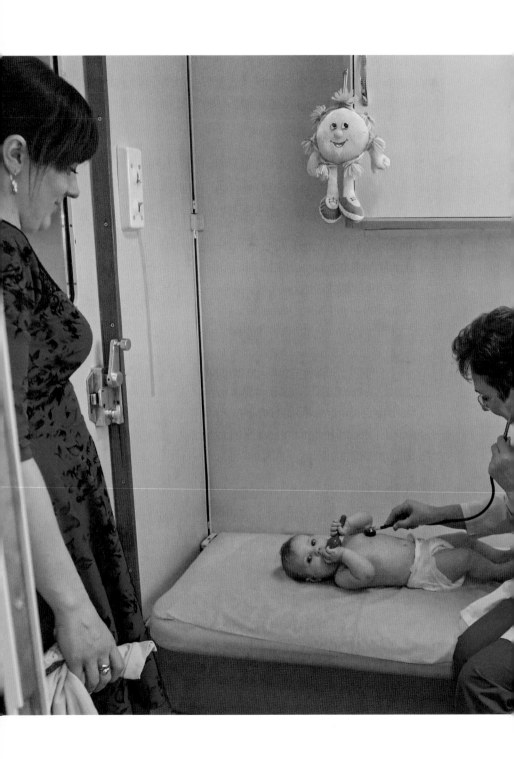

Health Care: Universal Right or Personal Responsibility?

was directed from Moscow. All programs were given goals to reach. Much of the allotted funds were spent each year on new facilities. But by the mid-1990s, the Soviet Union had collapsed. The republics were independent countries once again. The health-care system in Russia began to collapse as well.

Many factors contributed to the decline in Russian health care, such as contamination from nuclear accidents, overcrowded living conditions, a high rate of alcoholism, and a lack of new technology. The structure of the system itself also contributed to the fall. A specified treatment length was given to every illness or disease. As a result, a person with even a relatively light case of the flu, for instance, might be hospitalized instead of recovering at home. Hospital overcrowding was soon a fact. Poorly trained and poorly paid personnel hastened the decline. It was reported that about half of the country's doctors could not read an electrocardiogram (a graph of heart activity) when they graduated from medical school.

A doctor sees an infant patient in 2018 in a train that has been traveling through some of Russia's most remote areas in order to provide medical care there.

In 2006, the Russian government decided to take action. It announced it would increase spending on health care by taking funds mainly from oil revenues. The new plan called for high-tech medical centers, new equipment, and salary increases for doctors and nurses. It also shifted the emphasis from how many people were treated to how well they were treated.

Although Russia's deputy health minister called these changes of great benefit to the people, others had doubts. Commented Sergei Smirnov, head of the Institute of Social Policies and Social-Economic Programs: "How is it possible ... that a national health care project is managed not by the health ministry but by the presidential administration?" In the end, there is also still much to be done when it comes to costs. "On paper, Russian citizens are entitled to free universal health care," writes Marc Bennetts in *Newsweek*, referring to a provision of the Russian constitution. "In practice, however, they are required to take out compulsory private medical insurance, while it's also common for patients at state hospitals to bribe doctors for adequate treatment."

India

In 2018, the Indian government announced an ambitious plan to provide free health insurance to half a billion citizens. The plan has been nicknamed Modicare after Prime Minister Narendra Modi, whose government introduced the plan as part of the country's budget. The plan would allocate $188 million to build "health and wellness" centers and would cover costs of up to $7,800 for as many as 100 million low-income families. It also included significant investment in public health projects around tuberculosis, nutrition, cleanliness, and health education.

The plan, if implemented, would constitute the largest government-funded health-care program the world has ever seen. It would also spell a huge coverage expansion within

India, given that before Modicare, only 5 percent of Indians were covered—10 percent with private health insurance included. Today, many Indians still rely on traditional healers for their health care. This may be one reason that India's life expectancy was just 68 years in 2015, compared to 79 years in the United States and 76 years in neighboring China.

However, some doubt that this plan will be implemented, in large part because of the price tag, which will add up to several billion dollars. "How they're going to pay for this is puzzling all of us," Dipa Sinha, a New Delhi economics professor, told the *Washington Post* in February 2018.

Chapter Seven

THE FUTURE OF HEALTH CARE

What is the future of health care and health coverage in the United States? The Patient Protection and Affordable Care Act felt like a big step forward for many and continues to grow in popularity. However, many contingents in the US Congress, with the support of some of their constituencies, insist that the law is broken and needs to be revised. Others argue that it should be completely repealed, since government should have no role in regulating or providing health coverage for private citizens. The Affordable Care Act seems to stand on shaky ground, though on the other hand, a Republican-controlled Congress in 2017 couldn't manage to make significant changes to it.

Opposite: US senator John McCain speaks on the US Senate floor in July 2017 in a debate on the future of the Affordable Care Act.

In any case, the status of the Affordable Care Act is not the only factor to keep in mind as we look ahead to the future of health care in the United States and what further challenges the country may face.

Baby Boomers

Health care in America seems to have reached a crisis in large part due to the so-called Baby Boomers, the group of people born between 1946 and 1964, give or take a few years. Following World War II, there was an unusual spike in the country's birth rate. Now, according to estimates, about seventy-four million Baby Boomers are entering or already at retirement age. The oldest of them celebrated their sixty-fifth birthdays in 2011.

More and more, the Baby Boomers will need health-care services. By 2030, about 26 percent of the population will be sixty-five and older. However, there is more involved here than sheer numbers. In earlier decades, many older Americans relied on their families to care for them in their retirement years. That is largely no longer true. When the Baby Boomers were born, US families were more apt to be living close together. There were fewer divorces and more children. Also, the kinds of care are different today than yesterday. If a man survived a severe heart attack in the 1950s, for instance, the "cure" was probably bed rest for a few months and limited activity thereafter, which was probably not very long. Today, the same severe attack will likely be treated with surgery to repair clogged arteries and drugs to regulate blood flow. The result may well be a longer and more active life ... but the treatment is expensive.

In addition, Baby Boomers simply expect more. Senior Americans today often don't accept the old adage that pain or infirmity is a natural part of aging. They want medicines or

Support Programs

As the US population grows older and lives longer, health-care providers are trying to meet some of their needs by reaching out to the families and friends of older adults. Such programs not only help the elderly feel more supported, but offer guidance to caregivers who may have little or no experience caring for aging individuals.

One example of such a program is the Family Caregiver Support Program in Westchester County, New York, through the Department of Senior Programs and Services. The county has four full-service centers, including an Alzheimer's Association, and twelve resource centers in county libraries. The program includes spring and fall workshops that educate caregivers in available services throughout the county, a quarterly newsletter with important data for caregivers, and a staff that invites the caregiver to call or come in to talk about the problems of caring for the elderly.

Also included is help with a serious problem for many caregivers: what to do when an older driver insists on getting behind the wheel of a car. Other support programs in Westchester include a group for seniors older than sixty who are raising grandchildren of eighteen years or younger.

services that will keep them active and reasonably healthy well into their later years.

Faced with these prospects, it seems obvious that the current US health force cannot meet the requirements and expectations of aging Americans and at the same time take care of all others in medical need. Says John W. Rowe of the Mailman School of Public Health in New York, "We face an impending crisis as the growing number of older patients, who are living longer with more complex health needs, increasingly outpaces the number of health-care providers with the knowledge and skills to care for them capably." What to do?

Some health-care providers are planning now. The American Geriatrics Society says that more than 30,000 geriatricians will be needed by 2028. A geriatrician is a doctor especially trained to care for the health needs of older adults. The Summa Health System in Akron, Ohio, for instance, now offers two fellowship programs to train doctors of geriatrics. The program gives a year of clinical training and an optional year of research. Recognizing the growing need for future nursing services, DeKalb Medical Center in Georgia held a career fair for nurses in April 2008. It promised that all qualified candidates would get an interview and possibly a job. DeKalb listed the starting salary for new nurses at $47,000.

Shortages and Ailments

The real problem for health-care providers may be a shortage of primary-care physicians. Medical education costs, plus a desire for a better lifestyle, often lead medical school graduates into specialties in medicine, which pay more and tend to have better working hours. This trend makes it more difficult for patients to find primary-care doctors who, in turn, help them make better health-care choices. Some suggest opening medical schools to larger enrollments and focusing on primary care as a key part of the overall US health-care system.

Some experts in the medical field point to unhealthy lifestyle choices as the true culprit in our health-care problems. For one thing, too many Americans are overweight. Obesity drives up the costs of health care. The American Heart Association estimates that almost 70 percent of American adults are overweight or obese. Nearly one in three US children is overweight or obese. Overweight children and adults are at higher risk for heart disease, high blood pressure, high cholesterol, and type 2 diabetes. All of these conditions are expensive to treat and control.

Other health problems that increase the price of health care in America are heart disease, cancer, and stroke. These chronic diseases, along with injuries, are leading causes of death, and a great deal of health-care funding goes into the development of high-tech cures and techniques for addressing these conditions.

Addressing Costs

When it comes to the Affordable Care Act, supporters and detractors alike agree that premium costs are now too high, having more than doubled since the law took effect. Hillary Clinton ran on the Democratic ticket—the same ticket as Barack Obama and most Congressional supporters of the law—in the 2016 election, and she nonetheless took the position that remedying costs is a must.

Why have costs increased so much? First, experts say, it's important to make a distinction. Large-employer market prices are increasing at relatively normal, steady rates. Individual markets and those for small businesses are struggling much more with cost. Small businesses simply have smaller pools of people among whom to spread out risks and costs. Part of the reason for the individual

US senator Bernie Sanders, a former presidential candidate, speaks in support of universal health coverage at a 2017 convention in California.

market's struggle is uncertainty over the future of such markets, especially given repeated attempts to overhaul Obamacare in 2017. What's more, the Donald Trump administration has indicated it might end subsidies to insurance companies—price reductions that they usually pass along to consumers.

Whereas Republican Party members generally consider Obamacare to have gone too far in socializing medicine and introducing government into a central role in the health-care system, some argue it hasn't gone far enough. Senator Bernie Sanders insisted in September 2017 that a single-payer system was the best option: a system involving just one insurance provider—the government—rather than having multiple, competing insurance companies, referred to as a multi-payer system. "Instead of wasting hundreds of billions of dollars trying to administer an enormously complicated system of hundreds of separate insurance plans, there would be one insurance plan for the American people with one single payer," Sanders argued. This is often called a Medicare-for-All approach.

On the other side of the aisle, Republicans have not rallied behind a single solution. One suggestion from autumn 2017 negotiations, called the Graham-Cassidy proposal, suggested distributing money to states to use for health-care spending mostly at their own discretion. Large parts of the Affordable Care Act would be repealed, including the individual mandate, which requires that almost everyone have health insurance. Democrats, however, argue that the individual mandate is essential for keeping costs down, because it ensures that healthy people who don't use medical services much have to buy insurance as well as sick people, who use services more often. The Graham-Cassidy measure ultimately failed to pass.

The most dramatic moment in the months-long health-care debate of 2017 came on July 28, when Senator John McCain, who had just made an unexpected return to the Senate after being diagnosed with brain cancer, cast the deciding vote in a measure to repeal parts of the Affordable Care Act. McCain strode onto the Senate floor and stunned the room by indicating his vote with a thumbs-down. He joined two other Republicans in an otherwise party-line vote of 49–51. The Affordable Care Act was upheld.

That's not to say the law won't be challenged—in whole or in part—again and again. The debate rages on, not just on the Senate floor but in American homes, in newspapers and on television stations, in protests and marches and YouTube videos and Twitter feeds. With so many strong opinions and possible approaches at play, the debate may never be truly over.

Glossary

ambulatory care Medical care that takes place on an outpatient basis, such as in a doctor's office, and does not involve an overnight stay.

clinic A health facility providing outpatient care.

coinsurance Money that a patient must pay as his or her share of the cost of medical services after the patient has paid a deductible.

copayment The amount that the buyer must pay for a doctor's visit before the health plan kicks in.

deductible The amount an insured person pays for health-care services before his or her insurance plan starts to pay.

health insurance A plan that covers medical expenses in exchange for regular, scheduled payments.

health insurance company A business that offers health-care insurance coverage.

home health-care program A plan for individuals to receive health services at home.

hospital Usually a large facility that treats various medical problems, some on an outpatient basis, but most inpatient.

inpatient Receiving lodging and food as well as medical treatment.

Medicaid A US government health-care program for low-income people.

Medicare A US government health-care program for those sixty-five or older and people younger than sixty-five with special medical conditions.

nursing home A facility for those who need special or constant health care.

outpatient treatment Medical care not requiring an overnight hospital stay.

per capita Per person.

pharmaceutical company A commercial business that researches, develops, and markets health-care drugs.

pharmaceuticals Medicinal drugs.

premium The amount of money an individual pays for his or her health insurance each month.

prenatal clinic A facility, often for low-income patients, providing care and information for expectant parents.

preventive medicine A branch of medical science that focuses on preventing the occurrence of disease.

primary-care physician The doctor a person sees for basic medical needs.

Rx Abbreviation for "prescription."

surgicenter A specialty clinic where outpatient care is provided for minor surgeries.

Further Information

Books

Bradley, Elizabeth H., and Lauren A. Taylor. *The American Health Care Paradox: Why Spending More is Getting Us Less*. New York: PublicAffairs, 2013.

Brill, Steven. *America's Bitter Pill: Money, Politics, Backroom Deals, and the Fight to Fix Our Broken Healthcare System*. New York: Random House, 2015.

Dawes, Daniel E. *150 Years of ObamaCare*. Baltimore, MD: Johns Hopkins University Press, 2016.

Rosenthal, Elisabeth. *An American Sickness: How Healthcare Became Big Business and How You Can Take It Back*. New York: Penguin, 2017.

Sheen, Barbara. *Careers in Health Care* (Exploring Careers). San Diego, CA: ReferencePoint Press, 2014.

Websites

American Academy of Pediatrics

http://www.aap.org

The website of the American Academy of Pediatrics covers health issues, including those of adolescents and young adults.

Choose My Plate

http://www.choosemyplate.gov

This site offers tips on maintaining a healthy weight and lifestyle and helps you make smart food choices.

HealthCare.gov

http://www.healthcare.gov

Learn everything about how to enroll in health insurance, the difference between plan types, and how particular circumstances may affect health coverage.

Videos

Health Insurance Explained—The YouToons Have It Covered

https://www.youtube.com/watch?v=-58VD3z7ZiQ

This fun animated video from the Kaiser Family Foundation explains how health insurance works with the help of cartoon characters.

Introduction to the US Health Care System

https://www.khanacademy.org/partner-content/brookings-institution/introduction-to-healthcare/v/introduction-to-health-care

This video provides a great introduction to a complicated system by using the example of a single, hypothetical patient.

Why Is Health Care in the US So Expensive?

https://www.cnn.com/videos/health/2017/09/19/why-us-health-care-so-expensive-orig.cnn/video/playlists/your-health

This short video from CNN explains the factors contributing to high health-care costs.

Organizations

Commonwealth Fund

1 East 75th Street

New York, NY 10021

(212) 606-3800

http://www.commonwealthfund.org

This nonprofit organization is dedicated to improving the performance, quality, and efficiency of the health-care system.

Fraser Institute

4th Floor, 1770 Burrard Street,

Vancouver BC

Canada V6J 3G7

(604) 688-0221

http://www.fraserinstitute.org

The Fraser Institute produces key research on topics affecting quality of life in Canada, including health care.

Henry J. Kaiser Family Foundation

185 Berry St., Suite 2000

San Francisco, CA 94107

(650) 854-9400

https://www.kff.org

An authority on health policy analysis and journalism, this nonpartisan, nonprofit organization focuses on national health issues.

Patients Canada

65 Queen Street West, Suite 2010

PO #68

Toronto, ON M5H 2M5

(416) 900-2975

https://www.patientscanada.ca

This organization is dedicated to giving patients a voice in the health-care system.

St. Jude Children's Research Hospital

262 Danny Thomas Place

Memphis, TN 38105

(866) 278-5833

https://www.stjude.org

This hospital provides care and treatment for catastrophic illnesses to children, regardless of their families' ability to pay. The facility also conducts state-of-the-art research.

World Health Organization

Avenue Appia 20

1202 Geneva

+41-22-7912111

http://www.who.int

This agency of the United Nations works in more than 150 countries to fight diseases and collect important health-related data.

Bibliography

Abelson, Reed. "While Premiums Soar Under Obamacare, Costs of Employer-Based Plans Are Stable." *New York Times*, September 19, 2017. https://www.nytimes.com/2017/09/19/health/health-insurance-premiums-employer.html.

"Acute Lymphoblastic Leukemia (ALL)." St. Jude Children's Research Hospital, 2018. https://www.stjude.org/disease/acute-lymphoblastic-leukemia-all.html.

Angell, Marcia. *The Truth About the Drug Companies*. New York: Random House, 2004.

"Asthma Facts and Figures." Asthma and Allergy Foundation of America. Accessed March 18, 2018. http://www.aafa.org/page/asthma-facts.aspx.

Avorn, Jerry. *Powerful Medicines: The Benefits, Risks, and Costs of Prescription Drugs*. New York: Knopf, 2004.

Ballentine, Carol. "Taste of Raspberries, Taste of Death." *FDA Consumer*, June 1981. https://www.fda.gov/aboutfda/whatwedo/history/productregulation/ucm2007257.htm.

Barlett, Donald L., and James B. Steele. *Critical Condition: How Health Care in America Became Big Business and Bad Medicine*. New York: Doubleday, 2004.

Bennetts, Marc. "Russia's Bad Health Care System Is Getting Worse." *Newsweek*, November 21, 2016. http://www.newsweek.com/2016/12/02/dire-russia-health-care-523380.html.

Bowden, John. "Poll: Majority of Americans support ObamaCare." *Hill* (Washington, DC), August 11, 2017. http://thehill.com/policy/healthcare/346184-poll-majority-of-americans-support-obamacare.

Brend, Yvette. "We're Graduating More Doctors Than Ever, so Why Is It So Hard to Find a GP?" CBC, May 4, 2017. http://www.cbc.ca/news/canada/british-columbia/bc-doctor-shortage-medical-fees-1.4100251.

Carroll, Aaron E., and Austin Frakt. "The Best Health Care System in the World: Which One Would You Pick?" *New York Times*, September 18, 2017. https://www.nytimes.com/interactive/2017/09/18/upshot/best-health-care-system-country-bracket.html.

Christel, Michael. "Pharm Exec's Top 50 Companies 2017." PharmExec.com, June 28, 2017. http://www.pharmexec.com/pharm-execs-top-50-companies-2017.

Celgene Corporation. "Thalomid (thalidomide) NDA #020785: Risk Evaluation and Mitigation Strategy (REMS)." FDA.gov, August 2014. https://www.fda.gov/downloads/Drugs/DrugSafety/PostmarketDrugSafetyInformationforPatientsandProviders/UCM222649.pdf.

Centers for Medicare & Medicaid Services and National Association of Insurance Commissioners. "Choosing a Medigap Policy: A Guide to Health Insurance for People with Medicare." Medicare. gov, May 2017. https://www.medicare.gov/Pubs/pdf/02110-Medicare-Medigap.guide.pdf.

Cheney, Kyle. "Mass. Ditches RomneyCare Exchange." *Politico*, May 6, 2014. https://www.politico.com/story/2014/05/massachusetts-romneycare-health-care-exchange-106362.

Claxton, Gary, Cynthia Cox, Anthony Damico, Larry Levitt, and Karen Pollitz. "Pre-existing Conditions and Medical Underwriting in the Individual Insurance Market Prior to the ACA." Henry J. Kaiser Family Foundation, December 12, 2016. https://www.kff.org/health-reform/issue-brief/pre-existing-conditions-and-medical-underwriting-in-the-individual-insurance-market-prior-to-the-aca.

Coletta, Amanda. "Canada's Health-Care System Is a Point of National Pride. but a Study Shows It's at Risk of Becoming Outdated." *Washington Post*, February 23, 2018. https://www.washingtonpost.com/news/worldviews/wp/2018/02/23/canadas-health-care-system-is-a-point-of-national-pride-but-a-study-shows-it-might-be-stalled/?utm_term=.bcc6442a335f.

"Costa Rica—Health." Export.gov, July 31, 2017. https://www.export.gov/article?id=Costa-Rica-health.

Critser, Greg. *Generation Rx: How Prescription Drugs Are Altering American Lives, Minds, and Bodies*. New York: Houghton Mifflin, 2005.

Day, Eli. "The Number of Homeless People in America Increased for the First Time in 7 Years." *Mother Jones*, December 21, 2017. https://www.motherjones.com/politics/2017/12/the-number-of-homeless-people-in-america-increased-for-the-first-time-in-7-years.

DeNavas-Walt, Carmen, Bernadette D. Proctor, and Jessica Smith. "Income Poverty and Health Insurance Coverage in the United States: 2006." US Census Bureau, August 2007. https://www.census.gov/prod/2007pubs/p60-233.pdf

Doshi, Vidhi. "India Just Announced a Vast New Health Insurance Program. but Can It Afford It?" *Washington Post*, February 1, 2018. https://www.washingtonpost.com/world/asia_pacific/india-just-announced-a-vast-new-health-insurance-program-but-can-it-afford-it/2018/02/01/805efb46-0757-11e8-ae28-e370b74ea9a7_story.html?utm_term=.0be8dff64e8f.

Drum, Kevin. "A Very Brief Primer on Single-Payer Health Care." *Mother Jones*, July 1, 2017. https://www.motherjones.com/kevin-drum/2017/07/a-very-brief-primer-on-single-payer-health-care.

Ehman, Amy Jo. "Saskatchewan's 22-Month Wait for an MRI is 'Almost Criminal' Says Radiologists' Association." *Canadian Medical Association Journal*, March 2, 2004. http://www.cmaj.ca/cgi/content/full/170/5/776-a?maxtoshow=&HITS=10&hits=10

"Emergency Department Visits." Centers for Disease Control and Prevention, National Center for Health Statistics, May 3, 2017. https://www.cdc.gov/nchs/fastats/emergency-department.htm.

Farley, Tom, and Deborah A. Cohen. *Prescription for a Healthy Nation*. Boston, MA: Beacon, 2005.

"Financials." Howard Hughes Medical Institute, 2018. https://www.hhmi.org/about/financials.

Flowers, Aricka T. "National Market Could Cure America's Health Care Crisis: Policy Analysts." Heartland Institute, January 1, 2007. https://www.heartland.org/news-opinion/news/national-market-could-cure-americas-health-care-crisis-policy-analysts.

Gladwell, Malcolm. "The Moral-Hazard Myth." *New Yorker*, August 29, 2005. https://www.newyorker.com/magazine/2005/08/29/the-moral-hazard-myth.

Greider, Katharine. *The Big Fix: How the Pharmaceutical Industry Rips off American Consumers*. Cambridge, MA: Perseus, 2003.

Halvorson, George. *Health Care Reform Now!* New York: Wiley, 2007.

Harris, Gardiner. "Cigarette Company Paid for Lung Cancer Study." *New York Times*, March 26, 2008. https://www.nytimes.com/2008/03/26/health/research/26lung.html.

———. "CT Scans Cut Lung Cancer Deaths, Study Finds." *New York Times*, November 4, 2010. http://www.nytimes.com/2010/11/05/health/research/05cancer.html.

"Health Care Costs Main Cause of Personal Bankruptcy, Study Finds," *NewStandard*, February 4, 2005. http://newstandardnews.net/content/?action=show_item&itemid=1439

"Health Expenditures." Centers for Disease Control and Prevention, National Center for Health Statistics, January 20, 2017. https://www.cdc.gov/nchs/fastats/health-expenditures.htm.

"Health Insurance Coverage of Children 0–18." Henry J. Kaiser Family Foundation, 2018. https://www.kff.org/other/state-indicator/children-0-18/?dataView=1&currentTimeframe=1&sortModel=%7B%22colId%22:%22Location%22,%22sort%22:%22asc%22%7D.

"Health Insurance Coverage of the Total Population." Henry J. Kaiser Family Foundation, 2018. https://www.kff.org/other/state-indicator/total-population/?currentTimeframe=0&sortModel=%7B%22colId%22:%22Total%22,%22sort%22:%22asc%22%7D.

Higham, Scott, and Lenny Bernstein. "The Drug Industry's Triumph over the DEA." *Washington Post*, October 15, 2017. https://www.washingtonpost.com/graphics/2017/investigations/dea-drug-industry-congress/?utm_term=.256ea99ca898.

Himmelstein, David U., Miraya Jun, Reinhard Busse, Karine Chevreul, Alexander Geissler, Patrick Jeurissen, Sarah Thomson, Marie-Amelie Vinet, and Steffie Woolhandler "A Comparison of Hospital Administrative Costs in Eight Nations: US Costs Exceed All Others by Far." Commonwealth Fund, September 8, 2014. http://www.commonwealthfund.org/publications/in-the-literature/2014/sep/hospital-administrative-costs.

"Individual Adults." Washington State Health Care Authority, 2018. https://www.hca.wa.gov/free-or-low-cost-health-care/apple-health-medicaid-coverage/individual-adults.

"Inpatient Hospital Care." Medicare.gov. Accessed March 18, 2018. https://www.medicare.gov/coverage/hospital-care-inpatient.html.

"International Health Care System Profiles." The Commonwealth Fund. Accessed March 17, 2018. http://international.commonwealthfund.org.

Kaiser Family Foundation and Health Research and Educational Trust. "Summary of Findings." Employer Health Benefits 2007 Annual Survey, September 11, 2007. http://www.kff.org/insurance/7672/upload/76723.pdf.

Kalogredis, Vasilios J. "Should You Consider Concierge Medicine?" *Physician's News Digest*, February 2004.

Kauman, Marc. "FDA Says It Approved the Wrong Drug Plant." *Washington Post*, February 19, 2008. http://www.washingtonpost.com/wp-dyn/content/article/2008/02/18/AR2008021802315.html.

Kessler, R. C., et al. "Prevalence, Severity, and Comorbidity of 12-Month DSM-IV Disorders in the National Comorbidity Survey Replication." *Archives of General Psychiatry* 62, no. 6 (June 2006): 617–627.

"Key Facts about the Uninsured Population." Henry J. Kaiser Family Foundation, September 19, 2017. https://www.kff.org/uninsured/fact-sheet/key-facts-about-the-uninsured-population.

Khazan, Olga. "What's Actually Wrong with the US Health System." *Atlantic*, July 14, 2017. https://www.theatlantic.com/health/archive/2017/07/us-worst-health-care-commonwealth-2017-report/533634.

Klien, Ezra. "The Most Important Issue of This Election: Obamacare." *Washington Post*, October 26, 2012. https://www.washingtonpost.com/news/wonk/wp/2012/10/26/the-most-important-issue-of-this-election-health-reform/?utm_term=.a4d5ccfb1318.

Kliff, Sarah. "An Astonishing Change in How Americans Think about Government-Run Health Care." *Vox*, August 16, 2017. https://www.vox.com/policy-and-politics/2017/8/16/16158918/voxcare-poll-government-run-health-care.

Kuttner, Hans, and Matthew S. Rutledge. "Higher Income and Uninsured: Common or Rare?" *Health Affairs* 26, no. 6 (2007): 1745–1752.

Landa, Amy Snow. "Medicaid to Offer HAS Pilot Program." *American Medical News*, March 13, 2006. www.pnhp.org/news/2006/march/medicaids_health_op.php.

LeBow, Robert H. *Health Care Meltdown: Confronting the Myths and Fixing Our Failing System.* Chambersburg, PA: Alan C. Hood, 2003.

Luthra, Shefali. "'Concierge medicine' Is Reaching New Markets." *USA TODAY*, January 23, 2016. https://www.usatoday.com/story/news/2016/01/23/kaiser-concierge-medicine-reaches-new-markets/78814342.

Mahar, Maggie. *Money-Driven Medicine: The Real Reason Health Care Costs So Much.* New York: Collins, 2006.

"Malaria: Fact Sheet." World Health Organization, November 2017. http://www.who.int/mediacentre/factsheets/fs094/en.

Mangan, Dan. "Take a Look at the Maps That Show Obamacare's Big Effect on Americans' Health Insurance Coverage." CNBC, September 12, 2017. https://www.cnbc.com/2017/09/12/maps-show-obamacares-big-on-americans-health-insurance-coverage.html.

McAdams, Lisa. "Russia Readies Radical Health Care Reform." *Voice of America*, May 1, 2006, https://www.voanews.com/a/a-13-2006-05-01-voa31/398582.html.

McGreal, Chris. "How Big Pharma's Money—and Its Politicians—Feed the US Opioid Crisis." *Guardian* (UK), October 19, 2017. https://www.theguardian.com/us-news/2017/oct/19/big-pharma-money-lobbying-us-opioid-crisis.

Mechanic, David. *The Truth About Health Care.* New Brunswick, NJ: Rutgers University Press, 2006.

"Mental Illness." National Institute of Mental Health, November 2017. https://www.nimh.nih.gov/health/statistics/mental-illness.shtml.

Miller, Stephen. "For 2018, Expect Steeper Health Plan Premium Increases." Society for Human Resource Management, September 26, 2017. https://www.shrm.org/resourcesandtools/ hr-topics/benefits/pages/2018-health-plan-premiums-forecast. aspx.

Mishel, Lawrence. "Employers Shift Health Insurance Costs onto Workers." Economic Policy Institute, August 16, 2006. http:// www.epi.org/content.cfm/webfeatures_snapshots_20060816.

"Misuse of Prescription Drugs." National Institute on Drug Abuse, January 2018. https://www.drugabuse.gov/publications/ research-reports/misuse-prescription-drugs/how-many-people-suffer-adverse-health-consequences-misuse-prescription-drugs.

"Monitoring the Future 2017 Survey Results." National Institute on Drug Abuse, December 2017. https://www.drugabuse.gov/ related-topics/trends-statistics/infographics/monitoring-future-2017-survey-results.

"Most Republicans Think the US Health Care System is the Best in the World. Democrats Disagree." Harvard School of Public Health press release, March 20, 2008. https://www.hsph. harvard.edu/news/press-releases/republicans-democrats-disagree-us-health-care-system.

Mukherjee, Sy. "The GOP Tax Bill Repeals Obamacare's Individual Mandate. Here's What That Means for You." *Fortune*, December 20, 2017. http://fortune.com/2017/12/20/tax-bill-individual-mandate-obamacare.

National Coalition on Health Care. "Health Insurance Costs," National Coalition on Health Care. Accessed November 6, 2008. http://www.nchc.org/facts/cost.shtml.

O'Keefe, Ed. "The House Has Voted 54 Times in Four Years on Obamacare. Here's the Full List." *Washington Post*, March 21, 2014. https://www.washingtonpost.com/news/the-fix/wp/2014/03/21/the-house-has-voted-54-times-in-four-years-on-obamacare-heres-the-full-list/?utm_term=.001f5bacf3c7.

OECD. "Quality and Outcomes of Care: Avoidable Hospital Admissions." *Health at a Glance 2017: OECD Indicators*. OECD Publishing, 2017. https://www.keepeek.com//Digital-Asset-Management/oecd/social-issues-migration-health/health-at-a-glance-2017/avoidable-hospital-admissions_health_glance-2017-31-en#page1.

"Opioid Overdose Crisis." National Institute on Drug Abuse, March 2018. https://www.drugabuse.gov/drugs-abuse/opioids/opioid-overdose-crisis.

Park, Haeyoun. "We're Tracking the Ways Trump Is Scaling Back Obamacare. Here Are 12." *New York Times*, October 12, 2017. https://www.nytimes.com/interactive/2017/10/12/us/trump-undermine-obamacare.html.

"Pharmaceuticals / Health Products: Top Recipients, 2016."
OpenSecrets.org, Center for Responsive Politics. Accessed
March 19, 2018. https://www.opensecrets.org/industries/recips.
php?ind=H04&cycle=2016&recipdetail=P&mem=N&sortorder=U.

Ramsey, Lydia. "The Cost of an MRI Can Vary by Thousands of
Dollars Depending on Where You Go." *Business Insider*, March
28, 2017. http://www.businessinsider.com/how-much-an-mri-
costs-by-state-2017-3.

Ravsberg, Fernando. "Challenges and Realities of Cuba's Health
Care System." *Havana Times*, January 25, 2018. https://www.
havanatimes.org/?p=130072.

Reinberg, Steven. "Record Number of Americans Lack Health
Insurance," US News & World Report, August 8, 2007. http://
abcnews.go.com/Health/Healthday/story?id=4508456&page=1.

Reuters. "US prescription drug spending as high as $610 billion
by 2021: Report." CNBC, May 4, 2017. https://www.cnbc.
com/2017/05/04/us-prescription-drug-spending-as-high-as-
610-billion-by-2021-report.html.

Richmond, Julius B., and Rashi Fein. *The Health Care Mess: How
We Got into It and What It Will Take to Get Out*. Cambridge, MA:
Harvard University Press, 2005.

Rothman, Sheila M., and David J. Rothman. *The Pursuit of Perfection:
The Promise and Peril of Medical Enhancement*. New York:
Pantheon, 2003.

Roubein, Rachel. "Congress Repeals Obamacare Mandate, Fulfilling Longtime GOP Goal." *Hill* (Washington, DC), December 20, 2017. http://thehill.com/policy/healthcare/365785-congress-repeals-obamacare-mandate-fulfilling-longtime-gop-goal.

Sanders, Bernie. "Most Americans Want Universal Healthcare. What Are We Waiting For?" *Guardian*, August 14, 2017. https://www.theguardian.com/commentisfree/2017/aug/14/healthcare-a-human-right-bernie-sanders-single-payer-system.

Sanders, Katie. "Alan Grayson Claims 45,000 People Die a Year Because They Lack Health Insurance." *PolitiFact*, September 6, 2013. http://www.politifact.com/truth-o-meter/article/2013/sep/06/alan-grayson-claims-45000-people-die-year-because-.

Sarnak, Dana O., David Squires, Greg Kuzmak, and Shawn Bishop. "Paying for Prescription Drugs Around the World: Why Is the US an Outlier?" Commonwealth Fund, October 5, 2017. http://www.commonwealthfund.org/publications/issue-briefs/2017/oct/prescription-drug-costs-us-outlier.

Schmid, Randolph E. "Medical Care System Not Ready for Mass of Aging Baby Boomers." *AARP Bulletin Today*, April 14, 2008. http://bulletin.aarp.org/yourhealth/policy/articles/medical_care_system_not_ready_for_mass_of_aging_baby_boomers_study_says1.html.

Schneider, Eric C., Dana O. Sarnak, David Squires, Arnav Shah, and Michelle M. Doty. "Mirror, Mirror 2017: International Comparison Reflects Flaws and Opportunities for Better US Health Care." Commonwealth Fund, 2017. http://www.commonwealthfund.org/interactives/2017/july/mirror-mirror.

Scott, Dylan. "Why Donald Trump Makes Democratic Voters Uneasy about Medicare-For-All." *Vox*, February 8, 2018. https://www.vox.com/policy-and-politics/2018/2/8/16655796/democrats-medicare-for-all-clinton-voters-trump.

Sered, Susan Starr, and Rushika Fernandopulle. *Uninsured in America*. Berkeley, CA: University of California Press, 2005.

Stevenson, Jane. "Canadians' Health-care Costs Have Skyrocketed: Study." *Toronto Sun*, August 1, 2017. http://torontosun.com/2017/08/01/canadians-health-care-costs-have-skyrocketed-study/wcm/495190a8-ff3e-4016-aea2-43c61b4e6d3d.

St. John, Allen. "How the Affordable Care Act Drove Down Personal Bankruptcy." *Consumer Reports*, May 2, 2017. https://www.consumerreports.org/personal-bankruptcy/how-the-aca-drove-down-personal-bankruptcy.

Taylor, Jessica. "Mitt Romney Finally Takes Credit for Obamacare." NPR, It's All Politics, October 23, 2015. https://www.npr.org/sections/itsallpolitics/2015/10/23/451200436/mitt-romney-finally-takes-credit-for-obamacare.

Trefgarne, George. "NHS Reaches 1.4M Employees." *Daily Telegraph*, March 22, 2005. http://www.telegraph.co.uk/finance/2912588/NHS-reaches-1.4m-employees.html.

Trimble, Megan. "US Kids More Likely to Die Than Kids in 19 Other Nations." *US News and World Report*, January 11, 2018. https://www.usnews.com/news/best-countries/articles/2018-01-11/us-has-highest-child-mortality-rate-of-20-rich-countries.

"2016 National Healthcare Quality and Disparities Report." US Department of Health and Human Services, Agency for Healthcare Research and Quality, July 2017. https://www.ahrq.gov/sites/default/files/wysiwyg/research/findings/nhqrdr/nhqdr16/2016qdr.pdf.

US Department of Health and Human Services, Office of the Assistant Secretary for Planning and Evaluation. "Overview of the Uninsured in the United States: An Analysis of the 2005 Current Population Survey." Issue Brief, September 22, 2005. http://aspe.hhs.gov/health/reports/05/uninsured-cps/index.htm.

"US Drug Sales in 2007 Grow at Slowest Rate Since 1961." *USA TODAY*, March 12, 2008. http://www.laleva.org/eng/2008/03/us_drug_sales_in_2007_grow_at_slowest_rate_since_1961.html.

Weiss, Rick. "Study: US Leads in Mental Illness, Lags in Treatment." *Washington Post*, June 7, 2005. http://www.washingtonpost.com/wp-dyn/content/article/2005/06/06/AR2005060601651.html.

"What We Do: Budget." US Department of Health & Human Services, National Institutes of Health, March 6, 2017. https://www.nih.gov/about-nih/what-we-do/budget.

Winfield Cunningham, Paige. "The Health 202: Obamacare Was Supposed to Make CHIP Unnecessary." *Washington Post*, May 23, 2017. https://www.washingtonpost.com/news/powerpost/paloma/the-health-202/2017/05/23/the-health-202-obamacare-was-supposed-to-make-chip-unnecessary/59233963e9b69b2fb981db70/?utm_term=.449611b859d2.

Yeginsu, Ceylan. "N.H.S. Overwhelmed in Britain, Leaving Patients to Wait." *New York Times*, January 3, 2018. https://www.nytimes.com/2018/01/03/world/europe/uk-national-health-service.html.

Zur, Julia, MaryBeth Musumeci, and Rachel Garfield. "Medicaid's Role in Financing Behavioral Health Services for Low-Income Individuals." Henry J. Kaiser Family Foundation, June 29, 2017. https://www.kff.org/medicaid/issue-brief/medicaids-role-in-financing-behavioral-health-services-for-low-income-individuals.

Index

Page numbers in **boldface** are illustrations

AARP, 27–28, 87
Affordable Care Act (ACA), 5–7, 9, 13, 23, 31, 66–67, 73, 75, 77, 79, 81, 111–112, 115, 117
ambulatory care, 10–11, 62, 101
Australia, 7, 94

boutique doctor, 12–13
Bush, President George W., 23

Canadian health-care system, 32, 57, 70, 88, 94–95, 98
Centers for Disease Control (CDC), **50**, 52–54, 71, 83
Children's Health Insurance Program (CHIP), 23
clinic, 11, 13, 17–18, 20, 24–27, 48, 78, 80, 85, 95, 99, 104–105
coinsurance, 49
Commonwealth Fund, 6, 33, 83–84, 94
concierge medicine, 12–13

copayment, 12, 68–69, 78, 95
cosmetic surgery, 17, 105
Costa Rica, 11, 98–99
CT scan, 74
Cuba, 11, 99–100

deductible, 49, 68
Department of Health and Human Services (HHS), 27, 29, 41, 52, 54, 71
direct primary care, 13
Drug Enforcement Administration (DEA), 87–88

elective surgery, 15, 17
Elixir Sulfanilamide, 55–56, **56**
Emergency Medical Treatment and Active Labor Act (EMTALA), 80–81
emergency room (ER), 11–12, 16–17, 20, 33, 36, 46, 70–71, 76–77, 80
exclusive provider organizations (EPOs), 39

Federal Drug Administration (FDA), 54–58, 60–62, 89

France, 6–7, 32, 86, 94, 100–101

Germany, 32, 57, 94, 101

health-care aides, 13–14

health insurance, 6, 10–11, 23, 28, 34, 36, 40, 42–43, 45, 66–68, 73, 75–77, 79–80, 87, 93, 101, 104–105, 108–109, 117

health insurance company, 43, 68–69

health maintenance organization (HMO), 34–39

heparin, 60

home health-care program, 10, 14, 22

homeless population, 13, 77–78

hospice care, 10, 20–21

hospital, 6, 10–18, 21, 24, 27, 35–36, 38–42, 44, 46, 48, 51–52, 62–63, 68, 70, 80, 90, 95, 97, 99–101, 103–105, 107–108

India, 108–109

Indian Health Service (IHS), 27, 80

individual mandate, 10, 65, 117

inpatient,17, 68

Iran, 104

Japan, 7, 11, 104–105

Joint Commission, 62–63

Kaiser Permanente, 36–37

licensed practical nurse (LPN), 21

long-term care, 20–22, 44, 49, 62, 71, 95

managed care, 10, 34–35, 39

Medicaid, 7, 10, 20, 23, 25, 34, 40–45, 49, 66, 75, 88, 95

Medicare, 10, 12, 20–22, 28, 34, 39–45, 48–49, 63, 66–68, 71, 80, 87–88, 95, 117

medigap insurance policy, 43

mental health, 13, 23, 45, 48–49

multi-payer system, 31–32, 116

National Health Service (NHS), 10, 32, 101, 103

National Institutes of Health (NIH), 29, 84, 89

Native Americans, 27, 72

Netherlands, the, 6, 32, 94

nonprofit vs. for-profit, 14–15, 17

nursing home, 10, 20–21, **22**, 41, 44

Obama, President Barack, **8**, 9, 23, 65, 67, 115

Obamacare, 9–10, 13, 32, 65, 67, 116

Occupational Safety and Health Administration (OSHA), 52

opioid, 49, 88, 90

outpatient treatment, 12, 42

Patient Protection and Affordable Care Act (PPACA), 5, **8**, 9, 27, 65, 94, 111

per capita, 7, 32–33, **33**

pharmaceutical company, 10, 57, 84–87, 91

pharmaceuticals, 85

pharmacist, 13, 84

physical therapist, 14, **15**

point-of-service (POS) plans, 35, 39

preferred-provider organization (PPO), 35, 38–39

premium, 12, 28, 31, 34, 41–42, 45, 65, 68, 76, 79, 84, 115

prenatal clinic, 24–25

prescription costs, 6, 33, 69, 83–84, 87–88, 95, 98, 103

prescription drug abuse, 84, 89–91

preventive medicine, 51–52, 73

primary-care physician (PCP), 10–12, 35–36, 80, 114

registered nurse (RN), 14, 21

right to privacy, 5, 7

Russia, 105, 107–108

Rx, 86

Sanders, Senator Bernie, 31–32, 95, 116–117, **116**

single-payer system, 31–32, 116–117

social workers, 13–14, 49

special-interest group, 27–28

specialist, 6, 11–12, 36, 53, 100

subsidy, 7, 32–33, 93, 99, 116

substance abuse, 14, 49, 78

Supplemental Security Income (SSI), 44

surgicenter, 17

Switzerland, 32–33, 86, 94

thalidomide, 57–58

uninsured, 6, 22, 25, 33–34,
    69–70, 73, 75–77, 83, 94
United Kingdom, 7, 15, 32–33,
    70, 94, 101
United States Department of
    Veterans Affairs (VA), 26,
    80, 87
universal health coverage, 5, 7, 11,
    32, 66–67, 84, 93–95, 98,
    100–101, 103–104, 108, **116**
urgent-care center, 12, 20

Veteran's Health Administration
    (VHA), 26

World Health Organization (WHO),
    54, **92**, 100

About the Authors

Corinne J. Naden, a former US Navy journalist and children's book editor, is the author of more than one hundred nonfiction books for young readers, including *Political Campaigns* for the Cavendish Open for Debate series.

Erin L. McCoy is a literature, language, and cultural studies educator and an award-winning photojournalist and poet. She holds a master of arts degree in Hispanic studies and a master of fine arts degree in poetry from the University of Washington. She has edited nearly twenty nonfiction books for young adults, including *The Mexican-American War* and *The Israel-Palestine Border Conflict* from the Redrawing the Map series with Cavendish Square Publishing. She is from Louisville, Kentucky.